QUILT LOVE

The Taunton Press
Inspiration for hands-on living®

The Taunton Press, Inc., 63 South Main Street,
PO Box 5506, Newtown, CT 06470-5506
email: tp@taunton.com

First published in 2012 by **Jacqui Small LLP**
An imprint of Aurum Press Ltd
7 Greenland Street
London NW1 0ND

Library of Congress Cataloging-in-Publication Data

Ellis, Cassandra.
  Quilt love : celebrating events and telling stories
with contemporary patchwork / Cassandra Ellis ;
photography by Rachel Whiting.
    pages cm
  ISBN 978-1-60085-501-6
1. Patchwork--Patterns. 2. Quilting--Patterns. I.
Title.
  TT835.E466 2012
  746.46--dc23

10 9 8 7 6 5 4 3 2 1

Printed in China

Publisher Jacqui Small
Managing Editor Kerenza Swift
Commissioning Editor Zia Mattocks
Art Director Barbara Zuñiga
Photographer's Assistant
Corin Ashleigh Brown
Production Peter Colley

QUILT LOVE

SIMPLE PROJECTS TO STITCH & TREASURE

CASSANDRA ELLIS

Photography by Rachel Whiting

The Taunton Press

Contents

"Celebrate, commemorate, but most of all just *remember*: remember the *place*, the time, the life, or the person."

Threads

This is the **drawing together** of *threads*,
A **piecing together** of the **past** and the **future**,
A **time to stop** and *consider* where you've **been**,
where you're *heading*.

Quilts tell stories. The creation of precious patchwork tells of love, loss, friendships, and new beginnings. The act of piecing cloth together, to make something both practical and precious for you or yours, is an incredibly personal journey. Making quilts or smaller forms of patchwork is an opportunity to gather with friends or to work in solitude on something that will hold a lifetime of memories. It is a chance to take special fabric or clothing and weave a story from the threads of someone's life.

There are many reasons for making a quilt and many events in the course of a lifetime that are deserving. You may be starting a new life, or celebrating the new life of another. The joining together of two people is worthy of a quilt, as is the commemoration of a life well-lived. The loss of someone dear to you can be remembered with love, or a friend's broken heart can be healed with something you have made especially for them.

You may have a stash of precious cloth from your travels, or from markets or fabric stores. You may have held onto the dress from that summer vacation—the one that changed your life. You may have a scrap of your grandmother's wedding gown, or a dress that you wore as a child—memories, memories. When you handle these pieces, you remember, and this cloth weaves the threads of your life with the lives of others.

Many types of quilts have been made throughout history. Some were created out of necessity, some as an opportunity to show the maker's fine needlework and creativity. I believe quilts should show both the hand and the heart of the maker, so revel in your imperfections and personal style—imperfect is indeed perfect. Have confidence in your choice of colors and patterns. If you are making a gift for someone, think about them and what they love, but don't forget to put a bit of you into it— you are, after all, creating a story that weaves your threads together. If the quilt or patchwork is for you, think about your life and stories and what makes you happy.

Traditionally, making quilts provided an opportunity to sit with family and friends, talking, solving problems, or just being. These days, we are so busy and our leisure time is often taken up with TV or surfing the Internet, rather than creating something or enjoying easy company. We spend our lives rushing, yet most of our happy memories are of the slow times spent with friends or family, vacations, or big life changes. Celebrate, commemorate, but most of all just remember: remember the place, the time, the life, or the person.

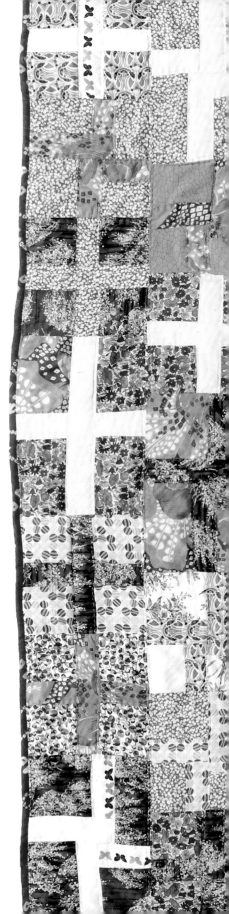

Big Events

Our lives are built on a series of events, the moments and decisions that pull us through to the next stage—birth, entering and leaving school or further education, first love, last love, jobs, no job, children, and grandchildren.

Every life is different and not all the markers will happen or be relevant to the life you choose. You may have children or you may be a Godmother, you might be married once or thrice, or never at all.

The key is to celebrate and commemorate your choices and the big events in your life and your family's lives by cutting and piecing your own story together.

New Baby Quilt

The impending arrival of a new baby into the world is always a cause for celebration and a great reason for a gift.

There is, of course, a huge list of practicalities to deal with and a huge amount of equipment to buy. And you can guarantee that any new arrival will be greeted with a tsunami of cuddly toys, baby clothes, and knit hats.

So much is focused on the baby's arrival that we often forget about their roots and why they came about in the first place. Who they are and the person they will become is largely determined by their genetic make-up and, of course, their parents, who wanted, hoped, and dreamed of them before they existed. I thought it would be lovely to welcome a baby into the world with a quilt of their own—something that represents not just who they are, but where (and who) they have come from.

When I designed this quilt, I thought about DNA and how a baby is a mix of both its parents as well as its grandparents, aunts, uncles, and cousins—first, second, and third removed. It is amazing to watch children grow and see how mannerisms, height, hair, and even the way they walk reflect somebody in their extended family.

So, by putting the baby in the middle of the quilt and the two families on either side, there is the opportunity to represent and celebrate everyone's contribution.

Finished size

The finished quilt measures 35½ x 48in (90 x 120cm). This fits a crib and is a versatile size when the child grows older.

Note: Metric to imperial conversions are calculated to increments not less than ¼in. Please work consistently in one system (metric) or the other (imperial).

Quilt top

You will need approximately 2¼–2¾yd (2–2.5m) of fabric in total for this design. If you use the same fabric for both of the two sides, as I have with the white fabric, you will need approximately 1¾yd (1.5m) for these sections of the quilt.

Quilt backing

If you want just one piece of fabric on the back, you will need 1½yd (1.4m) of cotton at least 43in (110cm) wide. If you are piecing the backing, you will need approximately 1¾–2¼yd (1.5–2m) of fabric, depending on the fabric width. The backing can be made up of the leftovers from the front or you can use something different.

Quilt binding

You will need approximately ½yd (0.5m) of fabric. Again, you can use your leftovers or introduce another fabric.

You'll also need

Batting—a piece approximately 4in (10cm) larger all round than the quilt top.

Sewing thread—100 percent cotton all-purpose thread in a neutral color.

Quilting thread—100 percent cotton in a color of your choice.

The design

This quilt is simple to make: a baby's quilt shouldn't be complicated, but it should give plenty of opportunity to integrate lots of special fabrics—you will probably spend much more time gathering fabrics than you will actually making. Now is the time to ask the parents and grandparents for family baby clothes and blankets, pieces from many generations, so that you can represent everyone. Alternatively, you may want to use new fabrics for this quilt, or a mixture of old and new. If the quilt is a gift, find out if the baby's room is being decorated and in what colors, so that you can choose fabrics to enhance the room. It is best if all the fabric is cotton, because a baby's quilt needs to be very washable.

I decided to make this quilt in bright vintage colors with a cream backdrop, so it is modern but charming. I mixed together cotton florals and Indian kantha prints with organic hand-loomed cotton. The quilt feels beautifully soft—the backing is also organic cotton.

Piecing it together

This is a quilt you can cut and sew in an afternoon, but as each piece is longish and skinny, they can easily get lost or confused. It is a really good idea to clear a space big enough to lay the quilt out as you are making it. Push the furniture against the wall, if you need to, or set yourself up in a bedroom, so that you can lay each strip down on the bed in the correct order as you make it.

Gather your special fabrics together and decide what you would like to use and in which order. The focus is on the central strip (B), which represents the baby. The left- and right-hand sides are for your support fabrics. You may have some pieces that are so small it will dictate where you can use them; otherwise, find a combination that is visually pleasing. Decide if you are going to repeat any fabrics or have a random placement.

Cutting out

Referring to the diagram on page 15, start with row 1 and cut the three pieces required, remembering that your central piece is the key. All seam allowances are ½in (1cm) and are included in the measurements given. Lay these pieces out, and repeat for rows 2–24. Lay each row down in the correct order as you go, so that you can see the quilt forming. This gives you an opportunity to change any fabrics if necessary.

Sewing the pieces together

Sew the three pieces of the first row together. With right sides facing, join A1 to B1, and then join C1 to B1. Press the seams. Repeat for rows 2–24.

To finish the quilt top, simply sew the rows together with right sides facing, starting at the top and joining row 1 to row 2 and then work your way down. Press all the seams as you go, and your quilt top is complete.

A finishing touch

On my quilt I also decided to add extra pieces of fabric on some of the outer edges (see photograph on page 14). You can either do this by appliquéing over the top of your finished quilt top, or by adjusting the measurements of the pieces on the left- and right-hand sides to take the extra fabrics. This feature is an added extra and completely up to you to include or not include.

Making the quilt

First make the backing. Sew your chosen pieces of fabric together until you have a square at least 4in (10cm) larger all round than your finished quilt top. Or cut a single piece of cotton to that size.

Then make the quilt sandwich, following the instructions on page 128.

This small quilt is quick and simple to hand-quilt and I think it is the right finish for a baby's quilt. I chose to use a simple running stitch and I followed each of the seams approximately ¼in (5mm) away from the seam line. (See also page 131.)

Trim your quilt so that the edges are even. This makes attaching the binding much easier. Make and attach the binding, following the instructions on pages 132–3.

Finished size when trimmed and bound: 35½ x 48in (90 x 120cm)

	A	B	C
1	14¾ x 3in (37 x 7cm)	9 x 3in (22 x 7cm)	14¾ x 3in (37 x 7cm)
2	8 x 3in (20 x 7cm)	20¾ x 3in (52 x 7cm)	9¾ x 3in (24 x 7cm)
3	13 x 3in (32 x 7cm)	13 x 3in (32 x 7cm)	13 x 3in (32 x 7cm)
4	16 x 3in (40 x 7cm)	7 x 3in (17 x 7cm)	15½ x 3in (39 x 7cm)
5	11 x 3in (27 x 7cm)	16½ x 3in (42 x 7cm)	11 x 3in (27 x 7cm)
6	18 x 3in (45 x 7cm)	5 x 3in (12 x 7cm)	15½ x 3in (39 x 7cm)
7	14 x 3in (35 x 7cm)	13 x 3in (32 x 7cm)	11½ x 3in (29 x 7cm)
8	7 x 3in (17 x 7cm)	24½ x 3in (62 x 7cm)	7 x 3in (17 x 7cm)
9	14¾ x 3in (37 x 7cm)	9 x 3in (22 x 7cm)	14¾ x 3in (37 x 7cm)
10	5 x 3in (12 x 7cm)	24½ x 3in (62 x 7cm)	9 x 3in (22 x 7cm)
11	13 x 3in (32 x 7cm)	13 x 3in (32 x 7cm)	13 x 3in (32 x 7cm)
12	16¾ x 3in (42 x 7cm)	7 x 3in (17 x 7cm)	14¾ x 3in (37 x 7cm)
13	11 x 3in (27 x 7cm)	16½ x 3in (42 x 7cm)	11 x 3in (27 x 7cm)
14	7 x 3in (17 x 7cm)	24½ x 3in (62 x 7cm)	7 x 3in (17 x 7cm)
15	16½ x 3in (42 x 7cm)	9 x 3in (22 x 7cm)	13 x 3in (32 x 7cm)
16	9 x 3in (22 x 7cm)	22½ x 3in (57 x 7cm)	7 x 3in (17 x 7cm)
17	16½ x 3in (42 x 7cm)	9 x 3in (22 x 7cm)	13 x 3in (32 x 7cm)
18	9 x 3in (22 x 7cm)	22½ x 3in (57 x 7cm)	7 x 3in (17 x 7cm)
19	13 x 3in (32 x 7cm)	13 x 3in (32 x 7cm)	13 x 3in (32 x 7cm)
20	14¾ x 3in (37 x 7cm)	7 x 3in (17 x 7cm)	16¾ x 3in (42 x 7cm)
21	11 x 3in (27 x 7cm)	16½ x 3in (42 x 7cm)	11 x 3in (27 x 7cm)
22	16¾ x 3in (42 x 7cm)	5 x 3in (12 x 7cm)	16¾ x 3in (42 x 7cm)
23	13 x 3in (32 x 7cm)	13 x 3in (32 x 7cm)	13 x 3in (32 x 7cm)
24	7 x 3in (17 x 7cm)	24½ x 3in (62 x 7cm)	7 x 3in (17 x 7cm)

Marriage Quilt

Initially, I thought this was going to be a wedding quilt, as that is where marriage begins. Then I realized that a wedding is very different from marriage, and what I actually wanted to celebrate and commemorate was the longer, more difficult, but far more rewarding part—being married.

Marriage can sometimes be glamorous, but often it is very humble. Sometimes it is exciting, sometimes a little routine and humdrum. Priorities shift and change, and the two people change and grow, as well. There are happy times and hard times, and all the while you are traveling through your lives together.

This quilt can be a gift for a happy couple, or it can be something that you make for you and your beloved. There is room for glamour and for the simple pleasures, with the opportunity to twist and turn, in order to create something of beauty—a lot like marriage itself.

The design

This design is based on a quarter log-cabin, one of the most traditional quilt designs created. However, each square in my interpretation is a little off-center and idiosyncratic. Rather than creating a design that is just based on two people, I thought that it should reflect how marriage brings many people together—families join together and friends get to know each other, and even the choices you make about where you live and what you do can bring new groups of people into your lives.

I made this quilt for my mother, and fabric-wise the design started with a precious scrap from her wedding dress. I remember seeing the dress when I was a child and it was so beautiful—white silk embroidered with silver thread—I couldn't believe fabric like this existed. My mother is tiny, so the dress probably wouldn't have been worn again, and I loved the idea of starting this quilt with the start of her married life—which, of course, was the start of my own life. When I chose the rest of the fabrics, I thought about the

Finished size

The finished quilt measures 82½ x 82½in (210 x 210cm); each square measures 27½ x 27½in (70 x 70cm).

Note: Metric to imperial conversions are calculated to increments not less than ¼in. Please work consistently in one system (metric) or the other (imperial).

Quilt top

You will need approximately 6½yd (6m) of fabric. The middle segments of each square need to be 10¾ x 13in (27 x 32cm), so make sure that any special fabric you want to use is at least this size. The longest pieces you will need are 28½in (72cm). If you are making this as a gift, find out what the couple love and gather cloth from friends or family to make it really special.

Quilt backing

You will need approximately 5½yd (5m) of backing fabric, depending on the fabric width. This can be made up of the leftovers from the front or you can use something new.

Quilt binding

You will need approximately ½yd (0.5m) of fabric. Again, you can use your leftovers or introduce another fabric.

You'll also need

Batting—a piece approximately 4in (10cm) larger all round than the quilt top.

Sewing thread—100 percent cotton all-purpose thread in a neutral color.

Quilting thread—100 percent cotton in a color of your choice.

things my mother loves and the places she would like to visit. So in the quilt there are some beautiful block-printed cottons from India and lovely floral cottons from Liberty of London, a small piece of vintage black silk from an antiques market and, to finish it off, Japanese cotton and silks from a favorite fabric supplier in Kyoto.

This isn't a difficult quilt to make and the design, made up of nine individual squares, allows many people to work on it or just one. The center of each square is an opportunity to curate the special and most important pieces of cloth—it is definitely the place for your wedding dress and his waistcoat fabric, or maybe fabric from your parents' marriages. The rest of each square can be filled with fabrics old and new, whatever you love and know that you will still love in many years to come.

Piecing it together

You could plan this quilt in two ways. One, you could decide on the fabric layout of each square individually. This method would be ideal if different people are going to work on the quilt or if you want to be slightly more random in how it turns out. Two, you could plan the whole quilt in one go, deciding where every piece will end up. If you want to do it this way, trace the diagram on page 20 and use it as your planning tool. I often use coloring pencils to mark particular fabrics on the plan, to get an arrangement I like the look of.

Cutting out

Once you have decided on the best method for you, it is time to start cutting. All seam allowances are ½in (1cm) and are included in the measurements given on the diagram. Clear enough space so that you can lay out a whole square— a dining table would be perfect.

Cut one square at a time, starting from the center piece (number 1) and work out (number 2, then number 3, and so on). Lay the pieces down in the same order as shown on the diagram, so that you can see the square build as you go. This gives you a chance to adjust things as you see your composition come together.

Once you have cut a whole square, you can start to sew pieces together.

Tip for cutting and piecing
When cutting, it will look like your pieces won't fit together. Don't worry, this is just the seam allowance and everything will shrink down accordingly when sewn.

Making up a square

Again, start with number 1, your center piece. Piece number 1 to number 2 with right sides facing and sew them together, then piece number 2 to number 3, and so on, working from the center out, until you have sewn all 14 pieces together to form the finished square. Press the seams as you go to make sure they are flat and look perfect.

Once your first square is completed, make eight more.

Joining the squares together

When you have made all nine squares, lay them out in an order that works for you. You may have done this at the planning stage, but if not, take your time, as it is amazing how much the quilt can change just by moving squares or by twisting or turning one square around.

Once you have decided on the order, pin and sew each row of squares together with right sides facing, to form three rows of three. Press the seams. Then pin and sew each of the completed rows together to make a square, making sure you match the seams as you go. Press all the seams and your quilt top is complete.

Making the quilt

First make the backing. Sew your chosen pieces together until you have a square at least 90½ x 90½in (230 x 230cm) or 4in (10cm) larger all round than your finished quilt top.

Make the quilt sandwich, following the instructions on page 128.

Machine- or hand-quilt the sandwich. The different options are explained on page 131. I chose to have this quilt long-arm quilted for a little luxury.

Trim the quilt so that the edges are even. This makes attaching the binding much easier. Make and attach the binding, following the instructions on pages 132–3.

Let married life commence—may it be long and happy.

Patch size: 27½ x 27½in (70 x 70cm)

1. 10¾ x 13in (27 x 32cm)
2. 10¾ x 3in (27 x 7cm)
3. 3 x 14¾in (7 x 37cm)
4. 4 x 14¾in (10 x 37cm)
5. 15¾ x 3in (40 x 7cm)
6. 15¾ x 4in (40 x 10cm)
7. 3¾ x 19¾in (9 x 50cm)
8. 18½ x 3¾in (47 x 9cm)
9. 3 x 22½in (7 x 57cm)
10. 5 x 22½in (12 x 57cm)
11. 24½ x 4in (62 x 10cm)
12. 3 x 25½in (7 x 65cm)
13. 26½ x 3¾in (67 x 9cm)
14. 3 x 28½in (7 x 72cm)

Finished size when trimmed and bound: 82½ x 82½in (210 x 210cm)

Special Birthday Quilt

When you are 9 years old, turning 10 is so important you can barely breathe; 13 is another significant age, as are 18 and 21—the party seems like it will never end. Then comes 30, and suddenly you are grown-up—well, you think you are, because once you turn 40, you realize you probably weren't. And on it goes until, at some point, you start glancing backward as much as looking forward, remembering the achievements and low points, the happiness and sorrow, friendships, loves, travels, and quests.

We all like to be revered and respected, by ourselves as much as others, so to celebrate a key birthday is an occasion in itself. Whether you are making a gift for a 21-year-old daughter or a 50-year-old friend, there are stories to tell and their dreams to piece together.

The design

When I designed this quilt I thought about the key markers in my life. Some of them are small and poignant, others are large and life changing. I wanted to reflect how we are all made by our experiences, but that, hopefully, we still have many more great ones to come.

The fabric choices started with a silk scarf that my mother gave me when I was 30. I thought the colors would be a terrific starting point for a quilt—buttermilk, sand, green, and blue. I decided to use some plain textured Japanese silks in blues and greens, a few more vintage scarves, dupion silk in sand and gold, and simple polka-dot cottons to pull it all together.

This is a controlled design, but one that allows you to mix as many or as few fabrics as you like. Small pieces butt up against large ones, skinny against chunky. The quilt is designed as four replicated square segments, which makes it easy to create the size you want—one segment would make a throw to go over your lap, two would be great for a child's bed and four are perfect for a queen-size bed. It also means that different people can work on the quilt if you choose—for example, if your family is scattered

Finished size
The finished quilt measures 88 x 88in (220 x 220cm); each square segment measures 44 x 44in (110 x 110cm).

Quilt top
You will need approximately 6-6½yd (5½-6m) of fabric. There are six different-sized pieces in the design, so you can work out what you need relatively simply. If you are using mementos, such as dresses or scarves, work out what you can cut from these first, so that you make the most of them (take a look at my notes on this on page 124). Then you can buy or gather the other fabrics based on what you need. Depending on whether the quilt is going to be a surprise or not, find out if the recipient has anything special they would like to include, or if there is anything from the family that they would like to be used. Otherwise, just think about the person—what colors they love, art that inspires them, or places they like to visit.

Quilt backing
You will need approximately 5½yd (5m) of backing fabric, depending on the fabric width. This can be made up of leftovers from the front or you can use something new.

Quilt binding
You will need approximately ½yd (0.5m) of fabric. Again, you can use your leftovers or introduce another fabric.

You'll also need
Batting—a piece approximately 4in (10cm) larger all round than the quilt top.

Sewing thread—100 percent cotton all-purpose thread in a neutral color.

Quilting thread—100 percent cotton in a color of your choice.

around the world or if a group of friends can all manage to make one segment each and want to put in their individual contributions. It's up to you and your circumstances and, of course, the birthday boy or girl.

This is a relatively simple quilt to make, as there are only 20 pieces in each segment. You could easily make one segment in an afternoon, as long as you have everything you need on hand.

Piecing it together

As this quilt is made from four segments, it is really important to make sure that any special fabric is distributed throughout the whole quilt, so that your eye is led across the whole piece. A great tip is to trace the quilt diagram on page 27 and mark where you would like these pieces to be. Cut them out first and number them on the back with a pencil (for example, if you decide to use a special piece of fabric for piece C2 on the pattern, mark "C2" on the back of it), then cut out all the remaining pieces for the first segment.

Cutting out

Clear some space close to your cutting and sewing area to lay out your pieces as you cut them—a large table or a hard floor is perfect (make sure it is free from dust, or lay a clean sheet down first).

Cut your fabrics based on the small diagram on page 27 and pencil the corresponding number on the back of each piece. The simplest way is to start with A1 and work from there, but if you have already cut any special pieces, you may want to start with them and choose and cut the other pieces around them. All seam allowances are ½in (1cm) and are included in the measurements given next to the diagram.

Once you have cut a whole segment, you can start to sew the pieces together.

Building the blocks

The numbering system may seem a little random, but I promise it isn't: it helps you to build blocks as you sew everything together. Each block within the segment starts with a letter, followed by a number—for example, A1. Start by joining pieces A1 and A2—with right sides facing, pin and

then sew them together. Then press the seam. Following the diagram, add A3—pin, sew, and press, as before. Then add A4—pin, sew, and press. This block is now complete.

Continue in the same way with blocks B through E. As you sew and build each block, put them back in their correct position in the segment before you start the next one. When all five blocks are complete, make up the segment as follows.

Making the segments

Start by joining block A to block B—with right sides together, pin, sew, and press. Then join this to block C in the same way—pin, sew, and press. Join block D to E—pin, sew, and press. Join this to block A/B/C—pin, sew, and press. Your first segment is complete.

Make three more of these 44 x 44in (110 x 110cm) segments for a full-size quilt. Keep checking the diagram to make sure that you have the blocks in the right order.

Joining the segments together

Once you have finished all the segments, play around with the positioning of each one to decide which goes next to which and in what direction they face. There is no right way—it's whatever pleases you visually.

Pin the first two segments with right sides together, sew, and press. Pin the second two segments together, sew, and press. Finally, pin these two larger pieces together, making sure you line up the seams, and sew and press. Your quilt top is complete.

Making the quilt

First make the backing. Sew your chosen pieces together until you have a square at least 96 x 96in (240 x 240cm) or 4in (10cm) larger all round than your finished quilt top.

Make the quilt sandwich, following the instructions on page 128. Machine- or hand-quilt the sandwich. The different options are explained on page 131. I chose to have this design long-arm quilted, but it would look equally lovely hand-quilted.

Trim the quilt so that the edges are even. This makes attaching the binding much easier. Make and attach the binding, following the instructions on pages 132–3.

I think this quilt is ready for a party.

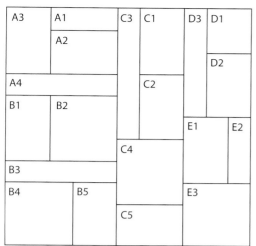

Segment size:
44 x 44in
(110 x 110cm)

A1. 13 x 5in (32 x 12cm)
A2. 13 x 9in (32 x 22cm)
A3. 9 x 13in (22 x 32cm)
A4. 21 x 5in (52 x 12cm)

B1. 9 x 13in (22 x 32cm)
B2. 13 x13in (32 x 32cm)
B3. 21 x 5in (52 x 12cm)
B4. 13 x 13in (32 x 32cm)
B5. 9 x 13in (22 x 32cm)

C1. 9 x 13in (22 x 32cm)
C2. 9 x 13in (22 x 32cm)
C3. 5 x 25in (12 x 62cm)
C4. 13 x 13in (32 x 32cm)
C5. 13 x 9in (32 x 22cm)

D1. 9 x 9in (22 x 22cm)
D2. 9 x 13in (22 x 32cm)
D3. 5 x 21in (12 x 52cm)

E1. 9 x 13in (22 x 32cm)
E2. 5 x 13in (12 x 32cm)
E3. 13 x 13in (32 x 32cm)

Note: Metric to imperial
conversions are calculated
to increments not less than
¼in. Please work consistently
in one system (metric) or the
other (imperial).

Finished size when trimmed and bound: 88 x 88in (220 x 220cm)

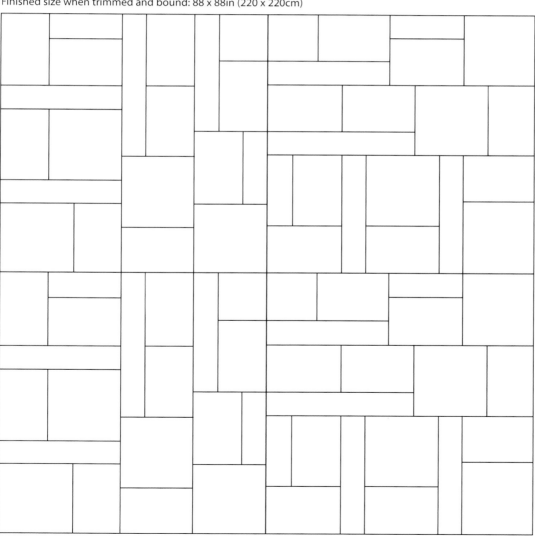

Don't forget that you
can rotate each segment
to get a composition
you like.

Leaving The Nest Quilt

I'm not sure whether leaving the nest is a greater wrench for the parents or the children. The latter are desperate for independence, but still need their parents to nurture and back them up. Half flying, half tethered to home and what home means, it is a big step to head off to college or your first apartment. Student rooms are generally not too pleasant—small and cramped, most definitely, and nine times out of ten, not likely to win an award for cleanliness. My mother was appalled when she saw my first home away from home: I craved freedom; she wondered how I could live in such an unattractive abode.

So, when they fly the nest, as well as food supplies, laundry back-up and cellphone credit, you can give them something that marks their first steps into adulthood. Something that will also add a personal touch to their first independent dwelling, with a welcome reminder of the comforts of home.

The design

I thought this quilt should be pretty simple—nothing complex, a light-hearted reminder of home. With three wide stripes, there is the option for you to pick something new, which reflects who they are now, while the medley of small stripes allows you to mix in some scraps from their past and maybe some from yours—a special dress, a coat, or a blanket that reminds them where they come from.

I find that if you choose the fabric for the wide stripes first, this is a terrific basis for selecting everything else, as it is easier to fit smaller pieces in tonally. However, if you have something small and really important to include, use this as your starting point—you never know where it might take you.

To form the three large segments, I started with a primrose-yellow feedsack cotton; the color is all about optimism and hope, and the print is simple but not childish—so perfect for this occasion. I also threw in a vintage pink woven ikat and a historic Liberty print.

Finished size

There are three size options: 59 x 83in (150 x 210cm); 71 x 83in (180 x 210cm); 83 x 83in (210 x 210cm).

Quilt top

You will need 4½-6½yd (4-6m) of fabric, depending on which size you choose to make.

Do make sure that, whatever size quilt you choose to make, you have pieces of fabric long enough to run the whole width (60in/152cm, 72in/182cm, or 84in/212cm). If you don't mind repeating a fabric, you will be able to get two of the wide sections out of one length. If you don't want to repeat fabrics, you can always use the leftovers for the backing.

For the skinny stripes, you can use pieces of fabric or clothing of any size, as long as you can get 2¼in (5cm), 3in (7cm), and 3¾in (9cm) widths out of them.

Quilt backing

You will need 4½-5½yd (4-5m) of backing fabric, depending on the size you are making. This can be made up of the leftovers from the front or you can use something new.

Quilt binding

You will need approximately ½yd (0.5m) of fabric. Again, you can use your leftovers or introduce another fabric.

You'll also need

Batting—a piece approximately 4in (10cm) larger all round than the quilt top.

Sewing thread—100 percent cotton all-purpose thread in a neutral color.

Quilting thread—100 percent cotton in a color of your choice.

Vintage embroidered cotton cloths, printed cottons, and soft linens in pink, orange, ivory, and green were mixed together to add interest to the skinny sections. To liven up the whole quilt, I chose an African wax-print cotton in a fun mix of pink, yellow, and orange for the backing fabric. I used the yellow feedsack cotton for the binding, to tie it all together.

Piecing it together

This is probably the fastest quilt to make in the book. The hardest part is curating the fabrics. Decide on the order of your three large pieces first. The fabric in the middle will be the most dominant when the quilt is finished.

Cutting out

Cut the three large pieces to the measurements shown on the diagram on page 32. All seam allowances are ½in (1cm) and are included in the measurements given.

Create three areas on your work table for the different skinny widths required—2¼in (5cm), 3in (7cm), and 3¾in (9cm). Take all of your remaining fabrics and cut strips to these widths. You will make four rows of strips 2¼in (5cm) wide, six rows of strips 3in (7cm) wide, and six rows of strips 3¾in (9cm) wide. Each individual strip can be any length. Just make sure you have approximately the right amount of each width for the required number of rows. It is better to cut too much—you can always use it on the back or for the binding.

Tip for using fabrics with motifs
If you are using fabric with an embroidered or patterned motif, make sure you plan your cutting around the motif, rather than splicing it in half or losing it altogether.

Making the skinny strips

Make up four rows of 2¼in- (5cm-) wide strips. Choose individual pieces and join them together with right sides facing, pinning, sewing, and pressing as you go. Use short and long pieces, patterned and plain, in a sequence that pleases you. Continue until you have a row that is at least the width of the quilt plus the seam allowance (that is: 60in/152cm, 72in/182cm, or 84in/212cm)—slightly longer than the quilt width is better, as you can trim off the excess later.

Once you have made four 2¼in- (5cm-) wide strips, put them aside, and repeat the process to make up six rows of 3in- (7cm-) wide strips and, lastly, six rows of 3¾in- (9cm-) wide strips.

Joining the segments together

Now you are ready to piece the whole quilt together. Following the diagram on page 32, lay out the pieces of the quilt. Move the skinny rows around to get the order you like, trying to avoid vertical seams matching. This is why it is a good thing for each strip to be longer than required, so that you can move it along and play around with its position.

When you are happy with the layout, pin each row together one at a time and sew, then press the seam. Continue until you have joined all the rows together.

Trim off any excess length from the skinny rows to make the edges even. Your quilt top is complete.

Making the quilt

First make the backing. Sew your chosen pieces together until you have a piece at least 4in (10cm) larger all round than your finished quilt top.

Make the quilt sandwich, following the instructions on page 128.

Machine- or hand-quilt the sandwich. The different options are explained on page 131. I chose to hand-stitch this quilt, using a simple running stitch. I followed each of the seams approximately ¼in (5mm) away from the seam line. I then randomly stitched diagonal rows across the middle section and wavy rows across the other two large sections.

Trim the quilt so that the edges are even. This makes attaching the binding much easier. Make and attach the binding, following the instructions on pages 132–3.

Finished size when trimmed and bound: 59/71/83 x 83in x (150/180/210 x 210cm)
The quilt shown opposite is 59in (150cm) wide

Note: Metric to imperial conversions are calculated to increments not less than ¼in.
Please work consistently in one system (metric) or the other (imperial).

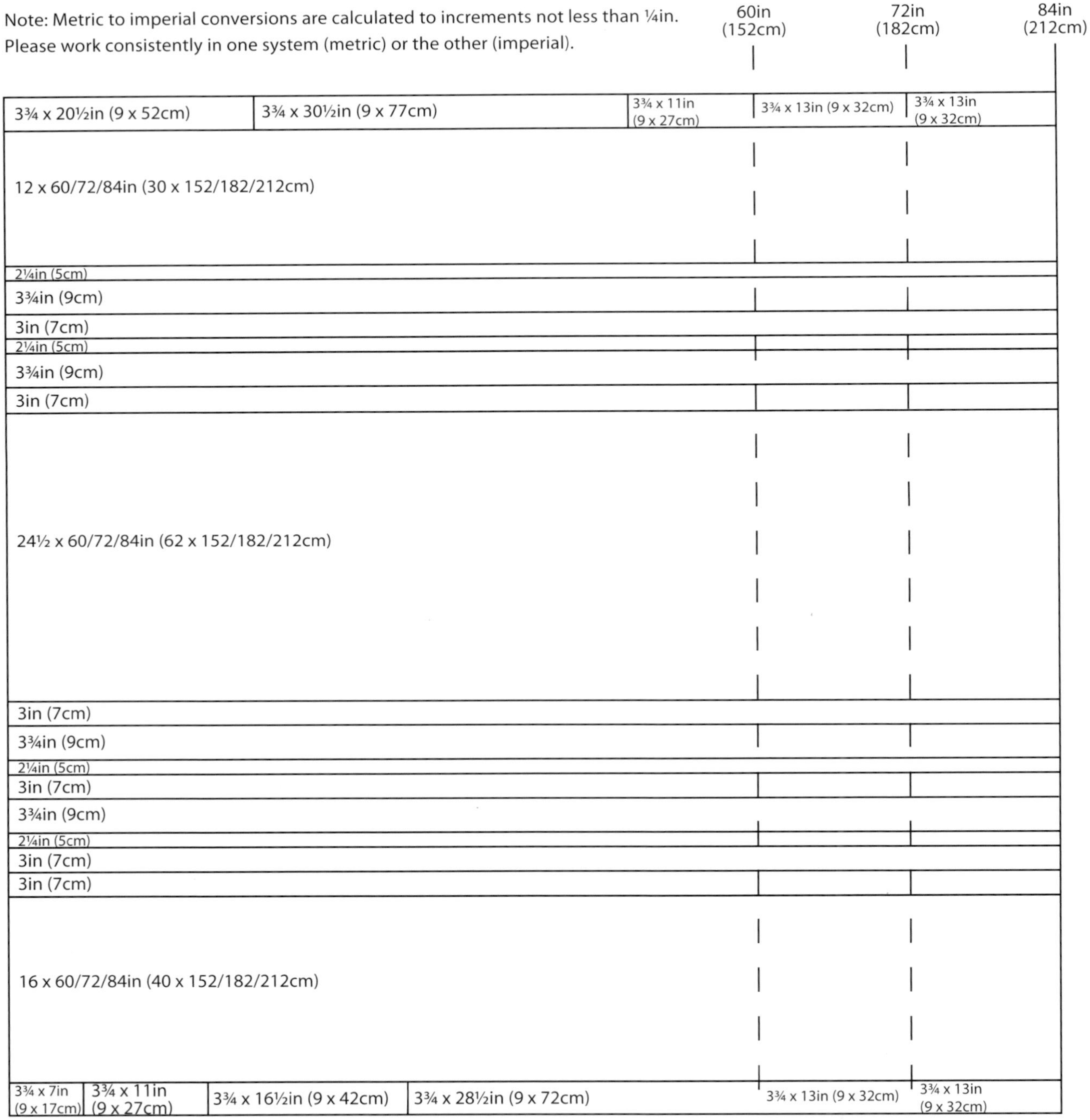

			60in (152cm)	72in (182cm)	84in (212cm)
3¾ x 20½in (9 x 52cm)	3¾ x 30½in (9 x 77cm)		3¾ x 11in (9 x 27cm)	3¾ x 13in (9 x 32cm)	3¾ x 13in (9 x 32cm)
12 x 60/72/84in (30 x 152/182/212cm)					
2¼in (5cm)					
3¾in (9cm)					
3in (7cm)					
2¼in (5cm)					
3¾in (9cm)					
3in (7cm)					
24½ x 60/72/84in (62 x 152/182/212cm)					
3in (7cm)					
3¾in (9cm)					
2¼in (5cm)					
3in (7cm)					
3¾in (9cm)					
2¼in (5cm)					
3in (7cm)					
3in (7cm)					
16 x 60/72/84in (40 x 152/182/212cm)					
3¾ x 7in (9 x 17cm)	3¾ x 11in (9 x 27cm)	3¾ x 16½in (9 x 42cm)	3¾ x 28½in (9 x 72cm)	3¾ x 13in (9 x 32cm)	3¾ x 13in (9 x 32cm)

Fresh Start Quilt

One of my first quilt commissions was from a woman who was getting divorced. It wasn't her choice, but it was happening anyway. Commissioning a quilt may seem like a strange thing to do in the midst of what was a very difficult time in her life, but she was determined to start her unplanned-and-unwanted-but-happening-anyway new life with a very positive gift to herself. It was one of the most joyous quilts I have ever made.

Making the quilt made me think about all the new beginnings we go through in life. We may encounter new jobs, cities, or countries, a new partner or the loss of one. Any of these changes can bring hardship and/or happiness. Being brave enough to tackle a new beginning is challenging, and I think these moments should be honored. It is not a reward per se, but a marker and a reminder of your fresh start once you are living your new life.

The design

Based on a traditional log cabin design, this quilt is a little wonky, a little off-center, which is generally how you feel when massive change comes upon you. The design starts from the center out—the first piece celebrating you or the person for whom you are making it.

The quilt is very simple and relatively quick to make, which is great for two reasons. Firstly, it will take your mind off your new day-to-day a little bit. Secondly, it means you can really go to town, spending time finding the perfect, and perhaps slightly indulgent, fabrics for your new beginning.

When choosing the fabric, start with the central piece and find something you adore. As you only need a small piece, this could justify an excursion to a textile fair or antiques market. Alternatively, you could pick a special piece you have had for years and have been waiting to use. Choose the other fabrics to tie in with the colors and patterns in the central piece. This is a quilt where you need to get to the stores and choose each fabric—I did use some fabrics that I had bought from

The finished quilt measures 84 x 84in (210 x 210cm). If you wish, you can make it smaller by leaving off the last few pieces or larger by adding more pieces.

Quilt top

You will need approximately 6½yd (6m) of fabric. If you like to repeat fabrics, you can mark out which fabrics will go where before you start, so that you know exactly how much of each fabric you need. If you prefer a more random approach, like I do, then it is likely that you will end up with more fabric than you need—you could use the extra for the backing, binding or for other projects.

The central piece is key and can be very special as it only needs to be 17 x 13in (42 x 32cm).

The longest strip you need to cut is 85in (212cm), so you will need fabric pieces up to that length. Alternatively, you can join pieces to form a continuous length, which would save on waste.

Quilt backing

You will need approximately 5½yd (5m) of backing fabric, depending on the fabric width. This can be made up of the leftovers from the front or you can use something new.

Quilt binding

You will need approximately ½yd (0.5m) of fabric. Again, you can use your leftovers or introduce another fabric.

You'll also need

Batting—a piece approximately 4in (10cm) larger all round than the quilt top.

Sewing thread—100 percent cotton all-purpose thread in a neutral color.

Quilting thread—100 percent cotton in a color of your choice.

eBay, there were more that didn't work once they arrived. As this quilt is about a new start, it is worth devoting the time to make sure every piece belongs there.

I wanted this to be a fresh, joyful quilt. For inspiration, I looked through a book on the French fashion designer Paul Poiret. I found a photograph of a very beautiful green, pink, and gold embroidered dress—and that was that. I bought a piece of heavily embroidered silk that became the center of the quilt, and everything followed from there. A couple of pieces of Liberty cotton, the lining and outer of a kimono, a strip of cotton velvet, and some bounty from the eBay purchases completed my selection. For the backing, I chose a woven African fabric that contrasts beautifully with the top.

Piecing it together

As there aren't many pieces in this design, each fabric becomes very important. How you place them next to each other and how you form a rhythm in the quilt will set the tone and mood of it. It is a good idea to have a planning and layout area next to your sewing machine. You may need to clear furniture so that you have ample floor space, or you can move your sewing machine to the bedroom and lay the pieces on the bed.

Tip for laying out fabric pieces
If you are going to use your bed to lay out your fabric pieces, strip it down to the mattress so that you have a flat surface to work on.

Work from the center out
Cut out your first precious central piece. Then lay it down in the center and start playing with the other fabrics, placing them next to each other and moving them around until you are happy. See how different colors and patterns set each other off. Vary scales, patterns, and colors to get a layout that you love.

Then, following the diagram on page 38, cut and join the pieces (with right sides together) in the order stated—that is, join piece 1 to piece 2, then add piece 3. All seam allowances are ½in (1cm) and are included in the measurements given on the diagram. Make sure you press with the iron every time you join two pieces together.

Don't cut everything at once for this quilt; just cut and sew as you go. This will allow you to make changes as your quilt grows.

Making the quilt

First make your backing. Sew your chosen pieces together until you have a square at least 92 x 92in (230 x 230cm) or 4in (10cm) larger than your finished quilt top.

Make the quilt sandwich, following the instructions on page 128.

Then machine- or hand-quilt the sandwich. The different options are explained on page 131. I chose to hand-stitch this quilt, using a simple running stitch. I followed each of the seams approximately ¼in (5mm) away from the seam line. I then randomly stitched around any large flowers or embroideries to add a bit of interest.

Trim the quilt so that the edges are even. This makes attaching the binding much easier. Make and attach the binding, following the instructions on pages 132–3.

And you are done. Time to toast your new beginning.

Finished size when trimmed and bound: 84 x 84in (210 x 210cm)

Note: Metric to imperial conversions are calculated to increments not less than ¼in. Please work consistently in one system (metric) or the other (imperial).

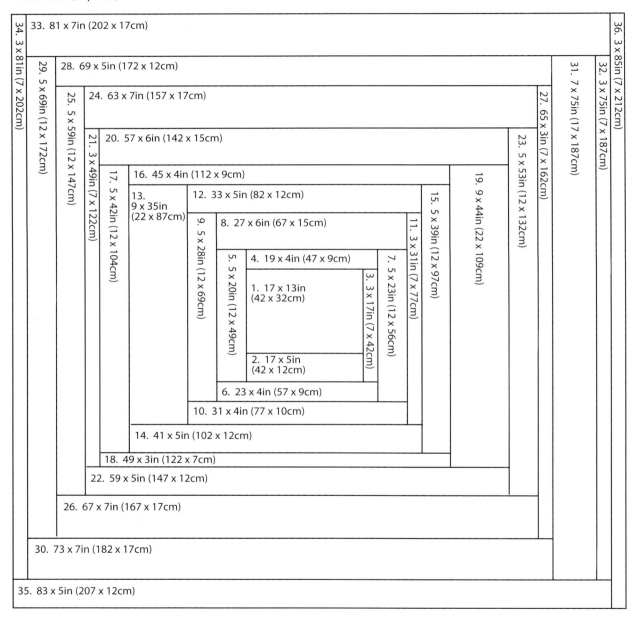

34. 3 x 81in (7 x 202cm)

33. 81 x 7in (202 x 17cm)

36. 3 x 85in (7 x 212cm)

29. 5 x 69in (12 x 172cm)

28. 69 x 5in (172 x 12cm)

32. 3 x 75in (7 x 187cm)

31. 7 x 75in (17 x 187cm)

25. 5 x 59in (12 x 147cm)

24. 63 x 7in (157 x 17cm)

27. 65 x 3in (7 x 162cm)

21. 3 x 49in (7 x 122cm)

20. 57 x 6in (142 x 15cm)

23. 5 x 53in (12 x 132cm)

17. 5 x 42in (12 x 104cm)

16. 45 x 4in (112 x 9cm)

19. 9 x 44in (22 x 109cm)

13. 9 x 35in (22 x 87cm)

12. 33 x 5in (82 x 12cm)

15. 5 x 39in (12 x 97cm)

9. 5 x 28in (12 x 69cm)

8. 27 x 6in (67 x 15cm)

11. 3 x 31in (7 x 77cm)

5. 5 x 20in (12 x 49cm)

4. 19 x 4in (47 x 9cm)

7. 5 x 23in (12 x 56cm)

1. 17 x 13in (42 x 32cm)

3. 3 x 17in (7 x 42cm)

2. 17 x 5in (42 x 12cm)

6. 23 x 4in (57 x 9cm)

10. 31 x 4in (77 x 10cm)

14. 41 x 5in (102 x 12cm)

18. 49 x 3in (122 x 7cm)

22. 59 x 5in (147 x 12cm)

26. 67 x 7in (167 x 17cm)

30. 73 x 7in (182 x 17cm)

35. 83 x 5in (207 x 12cm)

Joining Together Quilt

Joining together, coming together, being together: sometimes we get married, sometimes we don't, but the promise of saying "let's be together" is just as important. Choosing to be with someone and sharing the roof over your heads requires both emotional and practical commitment as well as compromise. Your precious furniture suddenly has to share room space with your partner's collection of guitars, and what is meant to be a romantic idyll can often become an emotional tussle over floor and wall space. However, what does happen as you share space and possessions is that you start to build a history of being together.

I love the idea of making a quilt that represents both of you—your Liberty print with his plaid shirt, or vice versa. You can make it together, or at least decide together on what is perhaps your first joint possession—and that should definitely overcome any furniture-versus-guitar disputes.

I wanted to reflect the thought of joining together in a different way for this quilt, so I decided to join cultures, too. This can be as perilous or as positive as a personal "coming together," but by focusing on the countries' united love for textiles, I thought that I could make something very special. I love the artisanship of indigo dyeing, so felt this would be a great opportunity to delve into different societies' execution of a time-honored technique.

The design

This design is so simple to make and it starts with the collaboration of you and your significant other. Even if you have completely contrasting styles, the simple strippy design allows seemingly disparate fabrics and patterns to exist comfortably side by side. Because each piece is relatively small and almost uniform in size, big patterns and small patterns, loud colors and muted colors

Finished size

The finished quilt measures 83 x 80in (210 x 200cm). You can make it as wide and long as you like: to up-size the quilt, just add more rows or strips to your rows; to make it smaller, just add fewer.

Quilt top

You will need approximately 6½–7¾yd (6–7m) of fabric for this design. More fabric is required for designs that are made up of lots of small pieces, as you lose the seam allowance every time you fire up the sewing machine.

The best place to start is with your own fabrics or clothing that each of you would like to contribute to the quilt (your individual pasts). Pile them together and see if there is a theme or colors that you both like (your present). Once you have this stash sorted, you can go shopping to fill in the gaps and pull the quilt together (your future).

Quilt backing

You will need approximately 5½yd (5m) of backing fabric for this size quilt, but remember to add more if you are making it larger. The backing can be made up of the leftovers from the front or you can use something new.

Quilt binding

You will need approximately ½yd (0.5m) of fabric. Again, you can use your leftovers or introduce another fabric.

You'll also need

Batting—a piece approximately 4in (10cm) larger all round than the quilt top.

Sewing thread—100 percent cotton all-purpose thread in a neutral color.

Quilting thread—100 percent cotton in a color of your choice.

will all meld together to create something that is really graphic and beautiful as well as extremely personal.

This quilt is built with a range of traditional indigo fabrics from India, Africa, and Japan, as well as modern chambray denim from America and indigo-colored prints from Liberty of London. I even dyed some fabric myself. To provide a bit of light relief, I included some hand-loomed ivory cotton. For the backing, I bought the most beautiful Ghanaian wax-print cotton—in indigo, of course.

Tip for using hand-dyed fabrics

When you are using hand-dyed fabrics, make sure you wash and wash and wash them until the water runs clear. A quick boil in salted water will help set the color.

Piecing it together

There are many, many pieces in this quilt, which can seem overwhelming, but if you break the project down into parts, it is actually really easy to make. The very first thing to do is to count the number of different fabrics you have. Then label up a corresponding number of large envelopes or plastic sleeves. I use envelopes as a way of containing cut pieces, sometimes because I don't have enough time to start sewing the quilt after I have cut it, but mostly because I am notoriously messy and they help keep me organized.

Cutting out

Cut your first fabric or item of clothing into 9in (22cm) strips (for tips on cutting up clothing see page 124). Then place each strip on your cutting mat and cut random widths—from 2–4¾in (5–12cm). You don't need to measure, as you will find you get into a natural rhythm of fat, fat, skinny, medium, medium, skinny, and so on. You will end up with pieces that measure 9in (22cm) long by 2–4¾in (5–12cm) wide.

Once you have finished cutting all of the first fabric, put the strips in an envelope and mark it: number 1 leopard print, or plaid shirt, as appropriate, depending on the material you have used. Continue doing this until you have cut all your pieces of fabric and put them in labeled envelopes.

Sewing the strips together

Take the fabrics from the envelopes and line them up. Pick one fabric and sew it to another, joining them along the 9in (22cm) length with right sides together; then add another and another. That's all you have to do. There is no right or wrong, and as you work you will find combinations that please you. Keep going until you think you are close to your required width, then press all the seams, as this will flatten out the strips and give you a true width. Continue sewing until you get to the width you want.

Then start on the next row and do the same. For this quilt, make ten rows 9in (22cm) long by 83in (210cm) wide. If some are slightly wider than this, you can trim the excess off at the end.

Joining the rows

Lay your rows out in an order that you like. You can use your bed or the floor for this, or pin them to a wall. This is a really important step and a great one to do together.

Starting at the top, pin two rows together with right sides facing. Pin heavily, as it will stop the rows from stretching and twisting, which they are prone to do in this kind of quilt. Sew the rows together, and repeat until you have attached all the rows. Press the seams and trim the excess, if necessary.

Making the quilt

First make your backing. Sew your chosen pieces together until you have a piece at least 91 x 88in (230 x 220cm) or 4in (10cm) larger all round than your finished quilt top.

Then make the quilt sandwich, following the instructions on page 128.

Machine- or hand-quilt the sandwich. The different options are explained on page 131. I chose to have this design long-arm quilted, as it helps to bring all the seemingly disparate pieces together. It also makes the quilt a little flatter, which I think works for this design.

Trim the quilt so that the edges are even. This makes attaching the binding much easier. Make and attach the binding, following the instructions on pages 132–3.

Finished size when trimmed and bound: 83 x 80in (210 x 200cm)

Note: Metric to imperial conversions are calculated to increments not less than ¼in. Please work consistently in one system (metric) or the other (imperial).

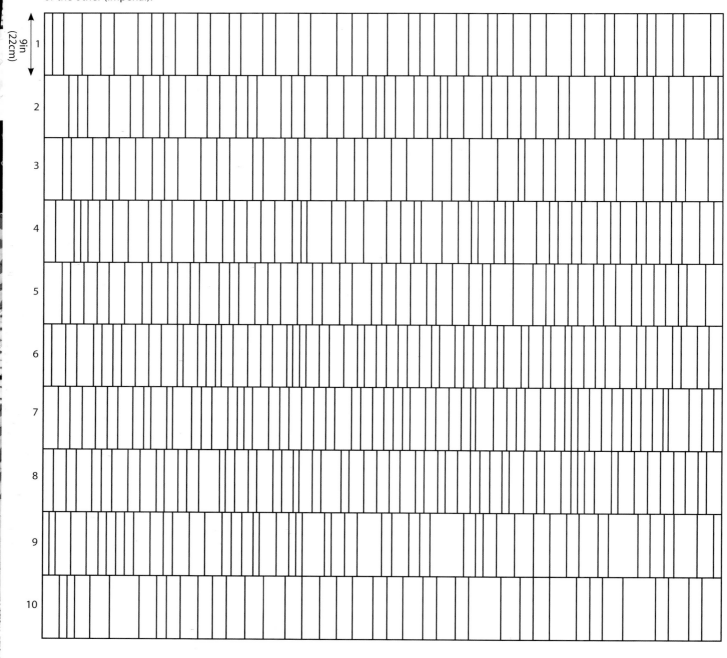

Love

It is often written that life is impossible without love. Yet there isn't just one kind of love, and the key to happiness seems to be finding, giving, and getting enough of all sorts. There is the head-over-heels love that most of us aspire to. Then there is love for family—sometimes easy, sometimes trying. There is love for our pets, who bring such joy yet demand so little. And there is love for friends, the people who choose to be in our lives. Perhaps most important is the love we give.

Love is a bond in whatever form it comes. I like to think of it as the thread that weaves, ties, and sometimes knots, yet always connects and (hopefully) never breaks.

I Love You Quilted Throw

Do you know someone who would love a beautiful throw to drape over their knees? Or perhaps you know a little girl who would like a doll blanket, or even a beloved dog or cat who deserves a pretty bed? I am sure you will answer yes to at least one of these questions.

Sometimes I make quilts by randomly piecing fabric together: rather than measuring, cutting, and stitching, I simply lay out a group of fabrics that I like and just go for it. It is incredibly liberating and amazing to discover how much beauty can come out of not thinking too hard.

I wanted to design a small project that could be made quickly, but that would also give you the chance to be a bit freer with your thinking. You have to trust your own design instincts and ideas, which is what I believe quilt-making should be about. I also wanted to demonstrate a different way of finishing and a different way of quilting.

The color schemes for these quilts were chosen from a scrap bag of Japanese silks that I bought at a fair. I love this method of buying, as you never know what treasures you are going to find. Sometimes, much of the fabric won't be to your taste, but at other times, it is like you have found textile nirvana. The scraps of silk in this particular stash came in ivory, slate, dusky pink, ocher, and navy—a beautiful combination that I may never have put together myself.

For the backing fabrics, I headed into my favorite fabric store and picked a selection of soft woven cottons—something a little sturdier to make the quilts more robust.

Finished size
This project will only work for small quilts—anything up to 47¼ x 59in (120 x 150cm).

Quilt top
Think about your fabric choices. If you are making this for your pet, silk will not be your best bet, but it would be lovely for your aunt. It is important to make sure that your choices are not only beautiful but also fit for the purpose, as you want your gift to be enjoyed for a long time.

Quilt backing
It is simpler to use one piece of fabric for the backing. Soft cashmere, woven cotton, velvet, or textured linen would all be lovely choices. The backing fabric needs to be 1in (2cm) bigger all round than your chosen finished size. So, decide on the dimensions of the finished piece and add another 1in (2cm) to the width and length. For example, for a throw measuring 23½ x 35½in (60 x 90cm), you need a backing piece measuring 24½ x 36½in (62 x 92cm).

You'll also need
Batting—one to four pieces 1in (2cm) smaller all round than the finished size. The number of layers of batting you use will give the quilt a different feel: four layers is great for a pet blanket, as it will be soft enough for them to lie on, whereas one layer will be perfect for a doll's pram.

Sewing thread—100 percent cotton all-purpose thread in a neutral color.

Embroidery thread in a color of your choice. Alternatively, you could also use wool, string, or fine strands of leather.

The design

First, decide on the size of quilt you want to make. This is completely flexible and depends on what or who you are making it for. Think about how many fabrics you want to use and if there are any particular sections of a piece of fabric that you want to highlight, such as a bird or a large flower.

Piecing it together

For this quilt, you need to start with the backing. Having decided on the finished size, cut out one piece 1in (2cm) larger all round than your chosen dimensions (see Quilt Backing, page 48). Use this backing piece as a template for your top piece.

Freestyling

Now the fun begins. Arrange your selection of fabrics until you have them in a layout that you like. Then you need to build blocks, by simply cutting and joining pieces together to create larger pieces. This is the same method as for most of the other projects in this book—the only difference is that there is no predetermined pattern or measurements to follow: I call it freestyling (see page 134). The only rule is that after you have sewn two pieces together, they both have to be the same length. If one piece is longer than the other, you will

need to trim off any excess before you join the next piece. You can see from the three throws shown here that I have used different size pieces and different layouts for each one.

Making the quilt top

All the seam allowances are ½in (1cm). Start by cutting, pinning, and sewing two pieces of fabric together with right sides facing. Press the seams. Then decide what fabric you want the next piece to be, where you want to join it, and what size you want it to be.

Continue cutting and joining pieces, using the backing as a template to ensure that you are heading for the right shape and size. What size each of the pieces are and in what order you join them is completely up to you. Make sure your completed quilt top is slightly bigger than your backing.

Making the quilted throw

Once you have finished piecing the top, press all the seams, and lay it right side up. Place the backing on top, right side down, and trim away any excess off the top piece so that both are the same size. Pin the two pieces together. Sew around three sides, leaving one of the shorter ends open. Press the seams, turn the quilt cover right side out, and press it again.

Cut one to four pieces of batting 1in (2cm) smaller all round than the finished size. The number of layers of batting you use depends on what you are making the throw for (see You'll Also Need, page 48). Lay the cut pieces of batting on top of each other and slide them inside the quilt cover. Make sure that the batting is completely flat and that you have inserted it right into the corners. Trim the batting if it is still too big. Then pin the unsewn seam closed with the raw edges turned inside. Hand-sew this side closed using a blind stitch.

All you need to do now is cross-stitch through the layers. On a practical level, this stitching will hold the three layers together, but it also gives you a chance for your last decorative flourish. This kind of quilting is more like tufting, but does exactly the same job as hand- or machine-quilting (see pages 131).

Using either an erasable pen or tailor's chalk, mark where you would like each cross-stitch to be. Using your chosen embroidery thread and a needle, simply sew through the quilt, making individual cross-stitches on your marked points. Clean off the chalk or pen marks, and you are done.

Comfort and Care Quilt

How often do we walk the streets of our cities and see someone who could use a little comfort? You may watch the news and see lives damaged or devastated. You might have a neighbor who has had sudden hardship or loss befall them. Somebody in your family might be having a difficult time. Or you may be involved with a charity that does great things, which makes you want to do something great, too.

Having somewhere comfortable and safe to sleep is something we all take for granted, but what about the homeless, the hurt, or the sad and lonely? Just imagine what a quilt could do for someone you know or don't know—but you know they need it. People everywhere need comfort and warmth.

The design

When I designed this quilt, I wanted to create something simple and relatively quick to make, but I still wanted it to be beautiful—uplifting, in fact. I also wanted it to be something that you can make on your own, or rally a group of friends together to make several in a day.

I chose colors that I knew would be both practical and visually nourishing. My starting point was a delightful fabric printed with glorious hydrangeas and butterflies, in rust, yellow, and blue. Colors affect how we feel and how we behave, so I really wanted to work with hues that have a positive effect—yellow for happiness, blue for calm, and rust for warmth. I then used simple plain cottons and linens, a vintage patchwork jacket, and some block-printed Indian cotton to tie it all together. For extra warmth I used rust-colored cotton corduroy for the backing, and for a bit of luxury, I bound the quilt with a strip of Indian silk sari.

This quilt is one of the simplest and fastest to make—as well as being an incredibly therapeutic project that is good for the soul. The design is simply built out of 12in (30cm) blocks, using randomly cut strips. It is a great quilt to use old clothing or fabric scraps for, but if you feel like buying new fabrics, then what a lovely reason to go shopping. If you are making the quilt (or quilts) with friends or colleagues, you can all bring clothing and fabrics and mix them together.

Finished size
The finished quilt measures 60 x 60in (150 x 150cm), but you can make it any size in increments of 12in (30cm): 60 x 72in (150 x 180cm) would cover a single bed and 84 x 84in (210 x 210cm) would cover a queen-size bed.

Quilt top
You will need approximately 5½yd (5m) of fabric or a bundle of clothes for this design. You only need to make sure each piece is a minimum of 13½in (33cm) wide.

Quilt backing
You will need approximately 4½–5½yd (4–5m) of backing fabric, depending on the fabric width. This can be made up of leftovers from the front or you can use something new. Alternatively, for this quilt, you could use a blanket, wool suiting, or fleece as the backing. If you do this, you won't need to use batting, which makes the quilt even simpler to make.

Quilt binding
You will need approximately ½yd (0.5m) of fabric. Again, you can use your leftovers or introduce another fabric.

You'll also need
Batting—a piece approximately 4in (10cm) larger all round than the quilt top—but remember, you won't need this if you use a blanket for the backing.

Sewing thread—100 percent cotton all-purpose thread in a neutral color.

Quilting thread—100 percent cotton in a color of your choice.

Piecing it together

The beauty of this quilt is the complete randomness of the fabric that you use—it is amazing how very different fabrics can work together. Start by pulling out all the fabrics and clothing that you have. Put combinations together until you find ones that you like. There is no defined number of fabrics that you should use—two or ten, it is up to you.

Tip for cutting up clothing

When using items of clothing to make a quilt, start by cutting off all the waistbands, collars, plackets, and cuffs. Then separate the pieces by removing the sleeves first, then the fronts from the backs. Press everything once you have done this. You now have lots of serviceable fabric to cut.

Cutting out

All seam allowances are ½in (1cm). Cut your first fabric or item of clothing into 13½in (33cm) squares. (You will find more advice on cutting fabric on page 124.)

Then you need to cut each square into strips. The fun bit is how you cut them. You don't have to cut all the strips a uniform width—you can cut on an angle to create irregular wedge-shaped strips. Try the following: cut one strip that graduates from fat to skinny, one that graduates from skinny to fat, and one that is straight up and down. You will find a rhythm as you work—the exact width of each strip isn't important, as long as you keep the 13½in (33cm) length.

Once you have cut all of one fabric, put the strips to one side (I suggest putting it in a labeled envelope if you are cutting lots of different fabrics). Then cut the rest of the fabrics using the same technique.

Now you are ready to start sewing the strips together.

Building the blocks

Choose your first two strips of fabric and pin and then sew them together with right sides facing. If you are joining two irregular-shaped pieces, make sure that the fat end of one is sewn to the skinny end of the other, otherwise your blocks will end up forming a circle rather than a square. Keep adding strips in an order that you like until your block is at least 13½in (33cm) wide.

Don't worry if your block looks a little off kilter. The extra fabric allowance in the length of the strips means that you can trim your finished block to the right size. Press all the seams on this piece and then trim it to 13 x 13in (32 x 32cm). This completes block 1.

Keep on piecing, pressing, and trimming until you have the required number of blocks. For this quilt you need 25 blocks.

Joining the blocks

Lay your blocks out in an order that you like, five across and five down to make a square. You can use your bed or the floor for this, or pin them onto a wall. This is a really important step.

In row 1, place the first block with the strips running vertically. Place the adjacent block with the strips running horizontally. Complete this row (a total of five blocks), alternating vertical with horizontal.

In row 2, place the first block with the strips running horizontally and the next block with the strips running vertically. Continue the row, alternating horizontal with vertical.

Continue in this way until you have laid out all of the blocks for your quilt.

Starting at row 1, sew the blocks together with right sides facing until you have a complete row. Press the seams. Repeat this for all the rows.

Starting at the top, pin and then stitch the first two rows together with right sides facing, making sure that you match each vertical seam. Repeat until you have attached all the rows. Press the seams and trim if necessary.

Making the quilt

First make your backing. Sew your chosen pieces together until you have a square at least 68 x 68in (170 x 170cm) or 4in (10cm) larger than your finished quilt top.

Make the quilt sandwich, following the instructions on page 128. Note: If you decide to use a blanket as the backing, you will not need to use batting as well and you will only need to join the quilt top to the blanket backing.

Machine or hand-quilt the sandwich. The different options are explained on page 131. I chose to machine-stitch this quilt in the seam lines of each block, as I wanted it to be quick and simple in execution, plus the size meant that it could easily be quilted on a domestic sewing machine.

Trim your quilt so that the edges are even. This makes attaching the binding much easier. Make and attach the binding, following the instructions on pages 132–3.

Perhaps the most rewarding part comes after you have made this quilt: it is time to give it to someone who needs it.

Finished size when trimmed and bound: 60 x 60in (150 x 150cm)

Note: Metric to imperial conversions are calculated to increments not less than ¼in.
Please work consistently in one system (metric) or the other (imperial).

Cheer Up A Loved One Table Runner

Many great memories come from sharing a meal, a piece of cake and a cup of tea, or a glass of wine around the kitchen table. Stories are told, laughter is shared, tears are dried, and sadness is comforted. When challenging things happen in our lives, we often bring and share food—it is what holds us together.

The kitchen table is invariably the heart of the home and I thought it would be wonderful to make a gift that celebrates this. A table runner will be brought out every time there is a special meal and will be at the center of many memories to come. Perhaps you will even have time to bake a cake to go with it.

Making this project is a fantastic way to use your creativity to pull something together, and it is also great practice before you move on to a full-size quilt.

Before you start, think about what colors or patterns the recipient loves and choose fabric to reflect this. Maybe incorporate something of theirs into your design, or see this as an opportunity to buy something new for them as your starting point. It is best if you stick to using cotton or linen fabrics, as a table runner will need to be washed on a regular basis.

The design

The inspiration for this runner came from the afternoon teas of my childhood. Growing up in New Zealand in the 1970s, everything was simple and seemed to be bathed in hazy sunshine. My mother baked every day and I loved coming home to ginger crunch, pikelets, or Anzac biscuits. I wanted this table runner to reflect those times. I mixed vintage linen with cotton feedsack prints, a couple of charming Liberty prints, and a tiny bit of ikat for a cheerful and sunny combination. For the back, I used my favorite ivory organic hand-loomed kantha cotton.

Finished size

The finished table runner is 16 x 79in (40 x 200cm), but it can be made any length you like. You could, in fact, make individual tablemats, if you prefer.

Note: Metric to imperial conversions are calculated to increments not less than ¼in. Please work consistently in one system (metric) or the other (imperial).

Table runner

For this size runner I used approximately 1½yd (1.25m) of scraps.

Table runner backing

I used a 17 x 80in (42 x 202cm) strip of cotton for the backing.

You'll also need

Sewing thread—100 percent cotton all-purpose thread in a neutral color.

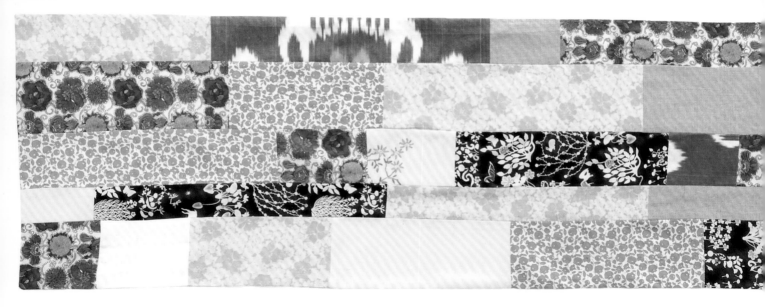

Piecing it together

This project uses a very simple stripping technique and is incredibly easy to piece together. Gather the fabrics that you want to use and think about how you want them to work together. What colors and textures do you want to juxtapose and what happens when you add or subtract certain pieces? Take your time with this, so that you are completely happy with your selection.

Cutting out

Start cutting out your pieces of fabric. As the diagram opposite shows, there are four different widths in the runner. All seam allowances are ½in (1cm) and are included in the measurements given. Starting with your first fabric, cut strips in all four widths until you have cut all that you want to use of that fabric. The length of each piece doesn't matter, but try to vary it from piece to piece.

Create a pile for each of the four widths and put your first fabrics down in these piles.

Continue cutting all the fabrics you want to use, varying the widths and lengths.

Once you have cut everything, shuffle each pile so that the order of the fabrics (not the sizes) are mixed.

Sewing the strips together

Starting with strip 1, pin and sew the short ends of two different fabrics together, with right sides facing. Continue adding pieces of the same width, picking different fabrics from that pile, to make up one long, skinny piece. Once you have reached the required length (or a bit more), press all the seams and put the strip to one side.

Refer to strip 1 as you piece the remaining four strips together in the same way.

Join the strips by pinning strip 1 to strip 2 with right sides facing and the top edges flush. Sew them together and press. Repeat this with strips 3–5 until you have the required finished width.

Trim the bottom end, so that you have the right length and a straight edge.

Making the table runner

Cut a piece of cotton or linen backing fabric to the same size as the patchwork top.

Pin the top to the backing, with right sides facing. Sew along all four edges, leaving a 6–8in (15–20cm) gap on one long side so that you can turn the table runner through to the right side. Press, and trim off the excess fabric at the corners. Turn the table runner right side out, making sure that the corners are sharp, and press again. Turn in and press the raw edges of the opening and slipstitch it closed.

Bake the cake or buy the quiche and you are ready for a bit more laughter around the table.

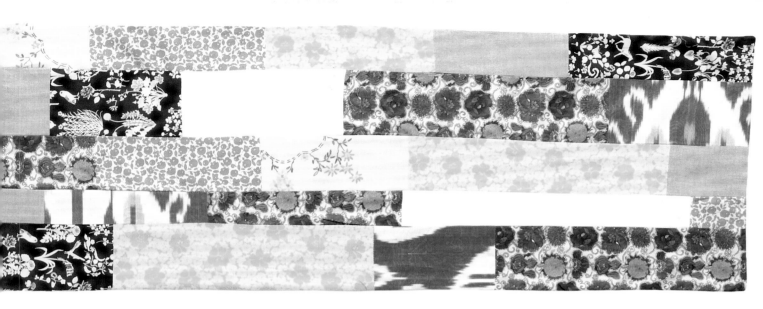

Finished size:
width: 16in (40cm)
length: adjustable

strip 1	strip 2	strip 3	strip 4	strip 5
3¾in (9cm)	5in (12cm)	4¼in (10cm)	3in (7cm)	5in (12cm)

Favorite Fabric Quilt

This is the quilt for anyone who has stashes of fabric hidden away in cupboards, trunks, or the attic—just about anywhere, in fact, that you can stash it.

There are usually pieces that aren't quite big enough for big projects you had planned, a swatch of something that you love, or even fabric for those drapes you never had time to make. It is likely that members of your family will bemoan the fact that it is invading their home and that you don't do anything with it. Don't feel guilty—this is the opportunity to turn your stash into something useful and beautiful.

If you are a true fabric collector, I am not even going to entertain the idea that you may not have enough fabric for this quilt, but if by some slim chance you don't, invest in something really fantastic—you only need a few large key pieces to make this quilt sing.

The design

The idea for this design was inspired by my love for Japanese kimono cloth. This type of fabric is only woven approximately 13in (33cm) wide and I couldn't bear to cut up these extraordinary patterns into small pieces, so I just started laying out each piece in its entirety. I kept adding other pieces next to and below the first piece, twisting and turning them until I found a layout I liked.

This quilt celebrates big pieces and bold statements. To make it work, make sure you balance any large prints with medium, small, and what I call no-prints—textured or woven pieces. Otherwise all those lovely large prints will shout at each other, rather than nestling together in harmony.

This quilt is very bright and joyful, with lots of red, orange, pink, and mint green. Adding ivory silk and some graphic patterns means you can see the birds soaring and the flowers blooming, which are quite magical to wake up to. The quilt is backed with soft organic cotton and bound with silk taffeta.

Finished size
The finished quilt measures 83 x 83in (210 x 210cm), but you can make this design in absolutely any size.

Quilt top
This is a tricky design to give exact quantities for, as it depends completely on your stash and the size of quilt you wish to make. For this size quilt, you will need approximately 5½yd (5m) of fabric.

Quilt backing
You will need approximately 5½yd (5m) of backing fabric, depending on the fabric width. This can be made up from more of your stash or you can use something new.

Quilt binding
You will need approximately ½yd (0.5m) of fabric. Again, you can use your leftovers or introduce another fabric.

You'll also need
Batting—a piece approximately 4in (10cm) larger all round than the quilt top.

Sewing thread—100 percent cotton all-purpose thread in a neutral color.

Quilting thread—100 percent cotton in a color of your choice.

Piecing it together

This quilt is based on the same principle as the "I Love You Quilted Throw" (see page 48)—that is, you are building blocks as for all other quilts, but with no predetermined pattern. If you prefer to plan your quilt design a little more methodically, see page 134, where I have explained how to design your own pattern.

Freestyling

Pull out all of your fabric and lay it out on the bed or floor. Select the fabrics that punch above their weight—those prints or colors that always make you smile. Position them on the bed roughly where you think you will use them in the design, and then work out which other fabrics you will use to balance and complement them. If you have some pieces that aren't quite long or wide enough, that's OK, just join on a strip of something else. Look at the photograph of the quilt opposite and you will see how all the different pieces fit together. Keep moving things around until you have a layout you are really happy with.

Tip for when you are freestyling

When making a large freestyle quilt, it is a great idea to take a photograph of your chosen layout. Firstly, as a visual prompt and secondly, just in case it gets moved.

Making the quilt top

Once you have everything laid out, it is time to start sewing. Using seam allowances of ½in (1cm) throughout, pin and sew two pieces together with right sides facing. Press the seams. If one piece is longer or wider than the other, you will need to trim off any excess before you join the next piece. Continue cutting and joining pieces, following your layout.

You may find that you need to add extra pieces or subtract pieces from your original layout—just take your time. You may find it easier to make three or four large blocks that you then join together into one large quilt. Just remember that the principle of building blocks is exactly the same, whether you have a precise pattern or you are creating your own.

Once you have reached the required size, press, trim off any excess, and make sure your quilt is "square."

Making the quilt

First make the backing. Sew your chosen pieces together until you have a square at least 4in (10cm) larger all round than your finished quilt top—in this case 91 x 91in (230 x 230cm).

Make the quilt sandwich, following the instructions on page 128.

Machine- or hand-quilt the sandwich. The different options are explained on page 131. I chose to have this quilt long-arm quilted, as I really like the way a more consistent pattern pulls all the different fabrics together.

Trim your quilt so that the edges are even. This makes attaching the binding much easier. Make and attach the binding, following the instructions on pages 132–3.

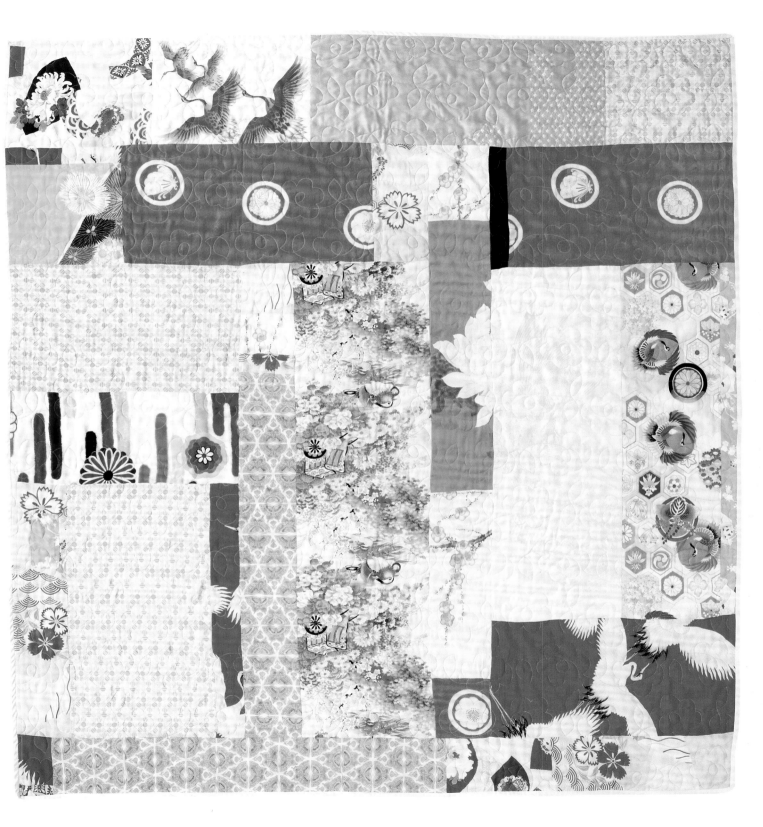

Friendship

Remember your first friend? How simple was it, as a 5-year-old, to just hug them and say "I love you?" As we grow up we make new friends through college, work, and hobbies, but as an adult it is not so easy to throw your arms around someone.

Whenever we encounter new places, interests, and loves, we connect with new people. We never know who we will become friends with or where that friendship may take us, and it can be just as magical as when we were children. We usually rely on our friends for different things—they may be our party pals, running mates, or choir buddies—and it is great to be able to celebrate the importance of friendship.

Friendship Bracelet

Making friends as an adult can be complicated. When life is busy, it is hard enough to fit in family and old friends, not to mention your partner's family and friends. But sometimes you meet someone and think, "Hey, I really like them." So, how do you actually tell someone you'd like to be friends?

The idea of a friendship bracelet has been around for some time: a tangible and tactile reminder of someone who thinks you are great. It is a wonderful idea to make them for special friends or new friends, and this design will work well whether you are 10, 30, or 60. Make them in private or with friends—preferably over cake and something lovely to drink.

Finished size
½in (1cm) wide and long enough to fit loosely around your wrist with a ½in (1cm) overlap.

You will need
Scraps of fabric—preferably silk, but any fabric could work.

Small piece of batting, approximately 12in (30cm) long—save your quilt scraps, or use fleece.

Embroidery thread in the color or colors of your choice.

Snap fasteners, one for each bracelet.

Sewing thread—100 percent cotton all-purpose thread in a neutral color.

The design

For these bracelets I raided my stash of silk scraps. I find it impossible to throw away any precious cloth and it was lovely to make something so beautiful from something so small.

Work out how long you need the bracelet to be. Use another bracelet as a guide, or measure your wrist and add ½–1in (1–2cm). Then decide on the width. I made these bracelets ½in (1cm) wide, but you could make them wider, more like a cuff.

Piecing it together

To start, cut a piece of batting (or fleece) to your chosen length and width (see above).

Cut scraps of silk ¾in (1.5cm) wider than the strip of batting and hand-sew or machine-stitch them together, end to end with right sides facing, until you have a piece 1in (2cm) longer than the strip of batting. Three or four different fabrics look lovely sewn together. I usually hand-sew the strips for ease, as it is super-quick and makes it a very portable project.

Cut a piece of fabric to the same length as your pieced strip. This will be the inside of your bracelet—the lining—so choose something that will contrast or complement the outside.

Making the bracelet

Press the seams on the pieced fabric strip. Lay the strip right side down and place the strip of batting centrally on top. Turn the short ends of the fabric strip over the batting and press. Then turn the long edges of the fabric strip over the batting and press. Set this to one side.

Turn in and press the short and long ends of the lining strip, so that they are the same size as the pieced strip. Lay this wrong side down on the batting and pin the three layers together, making sure that the pieces of fabric are the same size and the sides and ends meet exactly.

Choose embroidery thread in a complementary color and simply stitch around the edges to join the three pieces together.

Using cotton sewing thread, sew a snap fastener onto the ends of the bracelet—one part on the inside and the corresponding part on the outside. And you are done.

Morning Coffee Quilt Circle

One of the great traditions of quilting is that it was often done in the company of friends, family, and neighbors. Stories were told, recipes shared, and advice given, all while stitching and making. These groups created something practical and beautiful while enjoying each other's conversation and companionship.

It is so special when you get to have time out with friends—to gossip and giggle, away from the necessities and responsibilities of your daily life, if only for a few hours. Wouldn't it be wonderful to gather with these friends on a regular basis and make something very special together while enjoying each other's company? A modern day quilt circle, if you please. So don't hurry this quilt to completion—the longer you take, the more time you spend with your friends.

The design

This design is a little different to the other projects in this book. I wanted to create a pattern that was made up of small pieces of fabric, so the quilt top can easily be hand-stitched if you choose to. I also wanted the pieces to be small enough to enable friends to share, swap, and give treasured scraps of fabric to each other. This will make the time spent together even more enjoyable and ensure that you will remember it for years to come, every time you see that quilt.

When I chose the fabric, it all started with Liberty-print cottons. I wanted to use small but impactful prints in sophisticated colors and I think that Liberty does this best. I wanted the quilt to be dynamic and elegant, so I chose red, ivory, mulberry, and grassy green as the color palette.

By using small prints in small pieces, each block almost becomes graphic when stitched together, giving a modern feeling to traditional florals. I added in some plain cream kantha cotton and a few textured silks, so that I could define the crosses. For added luxury I used an antique silk sari for the backing, and I stripped the gold woven border off it to use as the binding.

Finished size
The finished quilt measures 64 x 64in (160 x 160cm), but you can change the size easily by choosing which blocks you use and how many.

Note: Metric to imperial conversions are calculated to increments not less than ¼in. Please work consistently in one system (metric) or the other (imperial).

Quilt top
You will need approximately 3¾yd (3.5m) of fabric for this quilt. As you are cutting smallish pieces, there will be very little waste. This is probably the one project in the book that you could use a whole bunch of fat quarters for, although that may take a little of the fun out of shopping for it. It is the perfect quilt to use up small scraps and loved mementos. If you are gathering with friends, you could all bring a few ½yd (0.5m) pieces each and share them around.

Quilt backing
You will need approximately 3¼yd (3m) of backing fabric, depending on the fabric width. This can be made up of leftovers from the quilt top or you can use something new.

Quilt binding
You will need approximately ½yd (0.5m) of fabric. Again, you can use your leftovers or introduce another fabric.

You'll also need
Batting—a piece approximately 4in (10cm) larger all round than the quilt top.

Sewing thread—100 percent cotton all-purpose thread in a neutral color.

Quilting thread—100 percent cotton in a color of your choice.

Piecing it together

This quilt is made up of 56 blocks— 16 of the 8 x 12in (20 x 30cm) rectangles and 40 of the 8 x 8in (20 x 20cm) squares. All seam allowances are ½in (1cm) and are included in the measurements given on the diagrams opposite. Remember, you can change the size of this quilt to suit you by adding or subtracting blocks (see the diagram on page 74).

First of all, decide whether you want to use the wonky crosses (A and C) or the symmetrical crosses (B and D)—or a mixture of both, which is what I did, because I like the way the irregular crosses lead your eye all over the quilt. Look at the photograph on page 75 and decide on how many of each.

With this quilt you can plan the placement of every block before you start making, or you can just make the required number of blocks and then lay them out at the end. I don't like to give only one option, as I know that some people like to plan everything at the beginning and some people don't.

However, if you are planning the whole quilt at the start, trace or copy the diagram on page 74 and draw in your crosses. Use coloring pencils to define different fabrics if this helps.

Cutting out

Starting with your 8 x 12in (20 x 30cm) blocks, you need to cut out the actual crosses first. Cut 16 crosses in total.

If you are using block A, cut out pieces 2, 4, 5, and 7 in one fabric.

If you are using block B, cut out pieces 2, 4, and 6 in one fabric.

Once you have cut a set, put it aside so that you can pick up the whole set when you start sewing (pop a pin through the pieces to hold them together if that helps).

Then cut the rectangles—you need 16 sets of these.

If you are using block A, cut out pieces 1, 3, 6, and 8 in one fabric.

If you are using block B, cut out pieces 1, 3, 5, and 7 in one fabric.

Again, once you have cut a set, put it aside so that you can pick up the whole set when you start sewing.

Then, cut your 8 x 8in (20 x 20cm) blocks in the same way, putting the pieces aside in piles as you cut them.

First, you need to cut 40 crosses.

If you are using block C, cut out pieces 2, 4, 6, and 7 in one fabric.

If you are using block D, cut out pieces 2, 4, and 6 in one fabric.

Then cut the squares/rectangles—you need 40 sets of these.

If you are using block C, cut out pieces 1, 3, 5, and 8 in one fabric.

If you are using block D, cut out pieces 1, 3, 5, and 7 in one fabric.

Making the blocks

With your sets of fabric laid out, you can choose which set of cross fabric to use with which set of square or rectangle fabric. Make up one block at a time, pinning and then sewing the pieces with right sides together in the order of the numbers given on the relevant diagram (that is, join piece 1 to piece 2, then join piece 3, and so on). Press the seams as you go.

Joining the blocks together

Once you have sewn all the blocks, you need to decide where you want to position each one. If you have already planned this, great; if you haven't, find enough space on the floor or bed to put the blocks down and move them around into an order that is pleasing. Look at the diagram on page 74 to make sure you have the right number and order of each size block in every row.

Create a row by joining the blocks in the first row end to end, pinning and sewing each one with right sides facing until row 1 is complete. Repeat this for rows 2–8. Press all the seams.

Pin rows 1 and 2 together with right sides facing; sew and press. Repeat this for rows 3–8. Press all the seams and your quilt top is complete.

Making the quilt

First make your backing. Sew your chosen pieces together until you have a square at least 72 x 72in (180 x 180cm) or 4in (10cm) larger all round than your finished quilt top.

Make the quilt sandwich, following the instructions on page 128.

Machine- or hand-quilt the sandwich. The different options are explained on page 131. I hand-quilted this design using a simple running stitch ¼in (5mm) away from each cross and around the outline of each block. This was a little time-consuming, so instead you could stitch diagonally across the quilt at intervals or just follow the outline of the blocks. This size quilt is also small enough to machine-quilt on a domestic machine.

Trim the quilt so that the edges are even. This makes attaching the binding much easier. Make and attach the binding, following the instructions on pages 132–3.

A

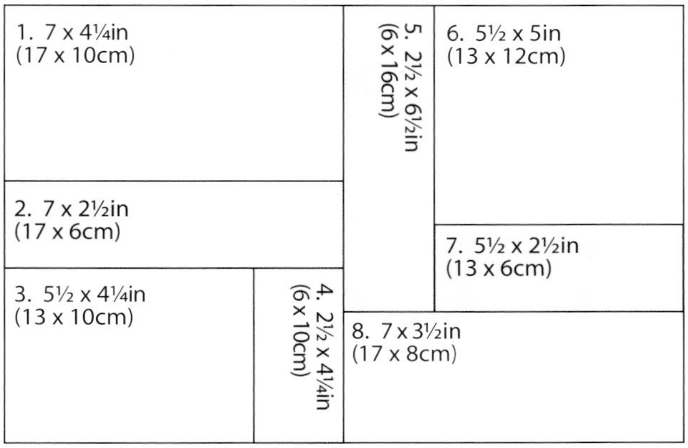

1. 7 x 4¼in (17 x 10cm)	5. 2½ x 6½in (6 x 16cm)	6. 5½ x 5in (13 x 12cm)
2. 7 x 2½in (17 x 6cm)		7. 5½ x 2½in (13 x 6cm)
3. 5½ x 4¼in (13 x 10cm)	4. 2½ x 4¼in (6 x 10cm)	8. 7 x 3½in (17 x 8cm)

B

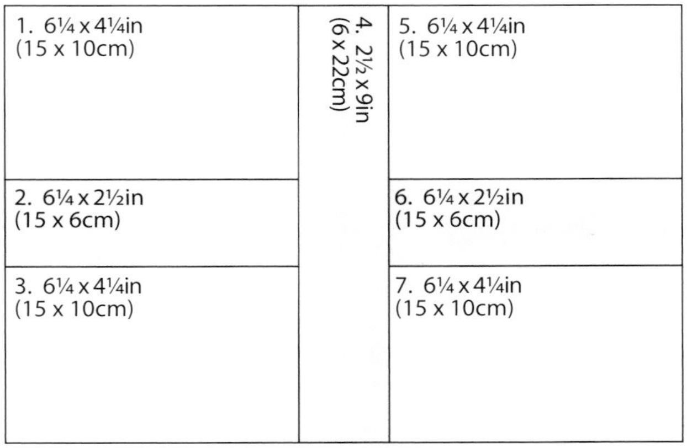

1. 6¼ x 4¼in (15 x 10cm)	4. 2½ x 9in (6 x 22cm)	5. 6¼ x 4¼in (15 x 10cm)
2. 6¼ x 2½in (15 x 6cm)		6. 6¼ x 2½in (15 x 6cm)
3. 6¼ x 4¼in (15 x 10cm)		7. 6¼ x 4¼in (15 x 10cm)

C

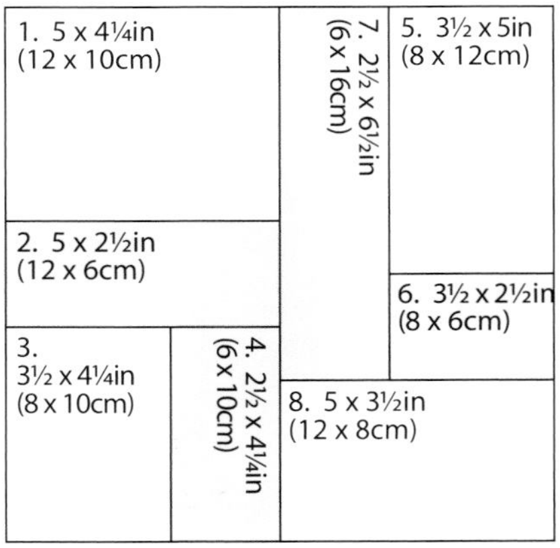

1. 5 x 4¼in (12 x 10cm)	7. 2½ x 6½in (6 x 16cm)	5. 3½ x 5in (8 x 12cm)
2. 5 x 2½in (12 x 6cm)		6. 3½ x 2½in (8 x 6cm)
3. 3½ x 4¼in (8 x 10cm)	4. 2½ x 4¼in (6 x 10cm)	8. 5 x 3½in (12 x 8cm)

D

1. 4¼ x 4¼in (10 x 10cm)	4. 2½ x 9in (6 x 22cm)	5. 4¼ x 4¼in (10 x 10cm)
2. 4¼ x 2½in (10 x 6cm)		6. 4¼ x 2½in (10 x 6cm)
3. 4¼ x 4¼in (10 x 10cm)		7. 4¼ x 4¼in (10 x 10cm)

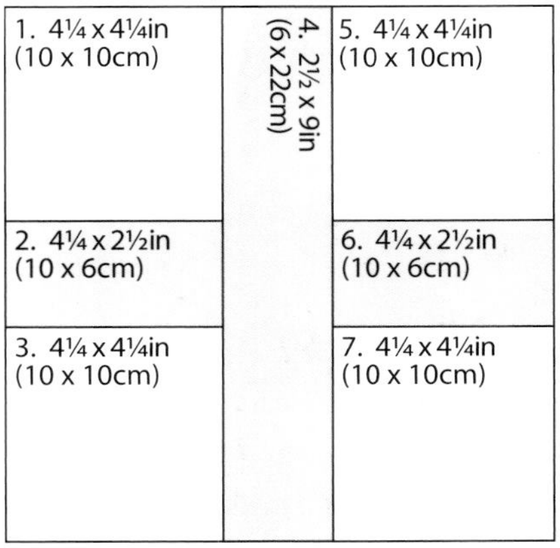

Finished size when trimmed and bound: 64 x 64in (160 x160cm)

A	D	B	D	C	D	C
D	C	D	B	C	D	B
A	D	B	D	C	D	C
C	D	C	A	D	B	D
A	D	C	A	C	D	D
C	D	C	D	B	D	B
A	C	D	A	C	C	D
D	C	D	B	D	D	A

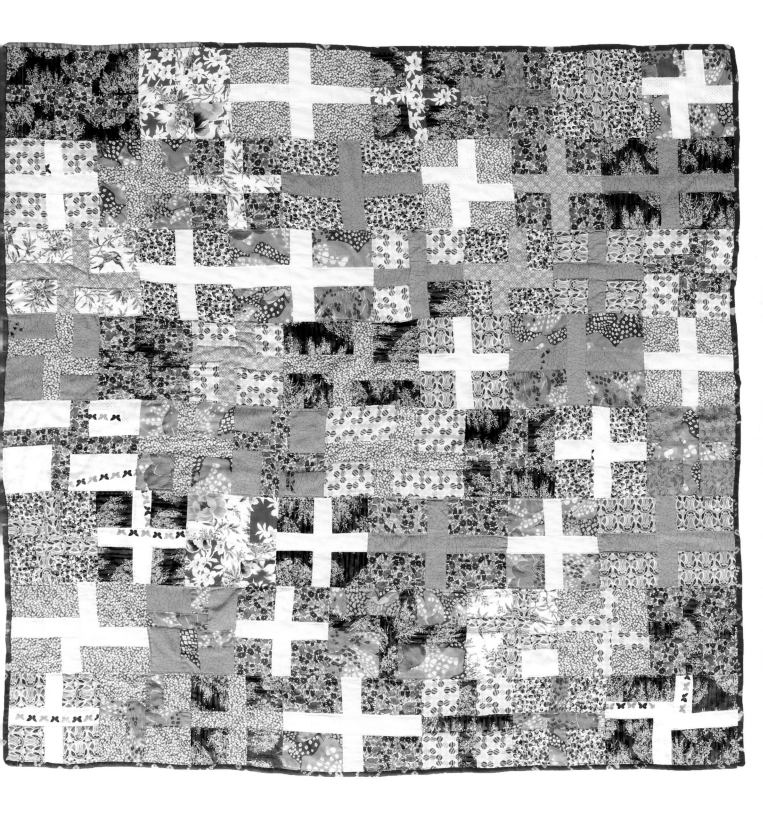

Catch-All Reversible Tote

A tote is a very useful thing, for everything from market shopping and carrying the baby's necessities to picnics and days at the beach. This reversible tote is almost ridiculously simple to make and is both a wonderful gift and a great treat for yourself. You could gather a group of friends together and make one each in an afternoon, or whiz them up as easy Christmas or birthday presents.

The design

This tote is on the large size, so it is perfect for groceries and diapers, towels, and swimsuits. The inner is made from one fabric and the outer from patchwork strips, which can be as contrasting or as simple as you like. (The design is reversible, but to avoid confusion when following these instructions, the patchwork is referred to as the outer.)

I wanted a tote that looked a little urban and quite cool with a hint of ethnic, which I would be happy to be seen carrying. I had been trying to find a way to use African mud cloth for one of the projects in this book, but it was too heavy for the quilts in both texture and pattern. It was, however, perfect for my tote. You need to choose strong fabrics, so wool cloths, canvas, or upholstery fabrics are great. Don't be tempted to use lighter cotton for a tote this size, as it could end in disaster. The rest of the strips are made from ivory canvas and black cashmere. The reverse side is washed Belgium linen—sounds delicious, doesn't it?

Piecing it together

First gather together the fabrics that you want to use and check that you are happy with the mix of colors and textures.

Making the straps
Use a tape measure to help you work out your desired length for the straps and cut four strips (see Tote Handles, above right). Turn in and press ½in (1cm) along both long sides of each piece. Pin two pieces together with wrong sides facing and the folded edges aligning. Topstitch them together along the two sides. Set your two straps aside.

Finished size
Height 15in (38cm); width 19in (48cm); depth 6in (16cm).

Note: Metric to imperial conversions are calculated to increments not less than ¼in. Please work consistently in one system (metric) or the other (imperial).

Tote outer
For the tote outer, you will need 16 strips of fabric each measuring 4 x 18in (10 x 46cm). You can use as few or as many different fabrics as you like.

Tote inner
For the tote inner, you will need two pieces of fabric each measuring 24 x 18in (64 x 46cm).

Tote handles
For the tote handles, you will need four strips of fabric 2½in (6cm) wide and 18–24in (45–60cm) long. The length of the handles is up to you, depending on how tall you are and whether you want to carry the tote in your hand or on your shoulder. Add an extra 4in (10cm) to your strap measurement, which will be sewn inside the bag for additional strength.

You'll also need
Sewing thread—100 percent cotton all-purpose thread in a neutral color.

Embroidery thread, linen string, or wool in a color of your choice.

Embroidery or darning needle.

Making the tote outer

For the outer, think about how you want the fabrics to work together. You can change the dynamic of the tote just by putting different fabrics next to each other.

With right sides facing, pin and sew together eight strips for each side of the outer using a seam allowance of ½in (1cm). Press the seams. Then, with right sides facing, pin and sew the two sides of the tote together along the two short sides and one long side (this will be the bottom of the tote).

Making the tote inner

With right sides facing, pin the two lining pieces together along the two short sides and one long side. Sew, leaving a 6in (15cm) gap in the long seam so that you can turn the tote through later. Press the seams.

Making the corners

Measure 7in (18cm) in from each side and mark the position of the handles on the top edges of the tote outer and inner. Pinch the bottom corners together to form a triangle 6in (16cm) across. Sew across this point on all four corners—two for the outer and two for the inner. This is what gives you the tote shape. Press as you go, as this will give you sharper edges.

Making the tote

Place the tote inner inside the tote outer with right sides facing. Place and pin the straps in between the right sides of the fabric at the marked points with the loops between the fabrics. Make sure you leave approximately 2in (5cm) of each end of the strap protruding beyond the raw edges of the tote, so there is no danger of them not being caught within the seam. Sew around the tote edge. Then turn the tote right side out through the gap in the seam of the inner. Turn in the raw edges of the opening and hand-stitch it closed. Press all the seams one last time, then push the bag inner inside the outer.

Your tote is finished, but you can add some decorative stitching to finish it off and to strengthen the handles.

Decorative stitching

Using an embroidery needle and your chosen thread, sew long running stitches or crosses through the tote outer, handles, and inner. I also hand-stitched at the base of the tote and where the triangle points meet (see below). A running stitch along each of the patchwork strips would be lovely, as would stitching around patterns on your fabrics, but it is completely up to you how much and where you embellish.

7in (18cm)   7in (18cm)

Tote inner—cut 2
24 x 18in (64 x 46cm)

Strips for tote outer—cut 16
4 x 18in (10 x 46cm)

Strips for tote handles—cut 4
2½ x 18–23in (6 x 45–60cm)

Housewarming Pillow

When friends or family move into a new home, it feels good to give them something handmade—something that reflects your relationship or your shared history. Moving home is stressful, both financially and emotionally, so a heartfelt gift is incredibly special and will be remembered for years to come. You could buy all new fabric, use special scraps, recycle clothes, or raid your other fabric stashes.

Making a quilt is quite a commitment, but a patchwork pillow is achievable and provides a great opportunity to use your innate creativity to pull something lovely together. It is also great practice before you move on to a more complicated and ambitious quilt.

The design

The design is based on a log cabin, but with a modern twist. This style of patchwork helps you with both the fundamentals of building blocks and in developing your intuition with color and pattern.

Find out what colors or patterns the recipient loves and choose fabrics accordingly. Maybe incorporate something of theirs into the design, or see this as an opportunity to find something new to use as the starting point.

For these pillows, I raided my fabric cupboard and used remnants from other projects—gorgeous pieces that I just couldn't throw away but that were too small for anything else. Although the design is the same, every pillow has a completely different feel, and all are very precious.

Piecing it together

Firstly, gather together the fabric that you want to use. It is best if you use fabric of similar weights, such as a cotton shirt with an old pillowcase. If you want to add in a silk or a knit fabric, feel free, just remember it will be a little harder to piece together, as knits and slippery fabric are more difficult to work with. Think about how

Finished size

There are two size options: 16 x 16in (40 x 40cm), a lovely size for a chair or as a feature piece, and 20 x 20in (50 x 50cm), which is ideal for a sofa or bed.

Note: Metric to imperial conversions are calculated to increments not less than $\frac{1}{4}$in. Please work consistently in one system (metric) or the other (imperial).

Pillow cover

For the front, you will need approximately 30in (75cm) of scraps. For the back, you will need between 20in (50cm) and 24in (60cm), depending on the size of the pillow.

You'll also need

Pillow form—these are readily and cheaply available from department stores or online. A feather filling is best, but use whatever you prefer.

Sewing thread—100 percent cotton all-purpose thread in a neutral color.

you want the fabrics to work together—which is the core fabric, which holds the most memories, what colors do you want to bring together? See what happens when you add or subtract certain fabrics: just one adjustment can completely change the look of the pillow. Take your time with this, so that you are completely happy with your selection.

Cutting out

Once you have ruminated and cogitated, start cutting out your pieces of fabric, following the diagram below. Start with piece number 1 and work outward to piece number 2, then number 3, and so on.

Lay the pieces in the correct configuration as you cut them out so that you can see the pattern forming. Pencil the number of the piece on the back, so that if you get interrupted or don't have time to finish the patchwork in one sitting, everything will be ready to go when you return.

Sewing the pieces together

As before, start with piece number 1. With right sides facing, pin and then sew number 1 to number 2, and then number 2 to number 3, and so on, working from the center out. Press the seams as you go.

Once you have finished sewing your pillow front, press it well all over. Then trim and square the edges, taking care not to over-trim.

Making the pillow back

Choose your backing fabric. This can be one complete piece, or you can sew leftovers from the front together to make up a piece large enough.

Press the backing fabric and lay it on your work surface right side up. Making sure it is flat, lay the pillow front on top with right sides together. Pin them together around all four edges and trim any excess fabric from the backing, if necessary.

Sew along three sides of the pillow cover and then sew 2in (5cm) in from both ends along the fourth side. Press, and trim the corners. Turn the pillow cover right side out and press the edges again.

Insert the pillow form. Turn in the ½in (1cm) seam allowance at the opening, and pin and then slipstitch it closed.

Wrap up the pillow, chill the champagne, and head on over to your friend's new home to celebrate.

For a 16 x 16in (40 x 40cm) pillow, cut pieces 1–9 only

For a 20 x 20in (50 x 50cm) pillow, cut pieces 1–13

Diagram:

12. 22 x 3in (54 x 7cm)
10. 3 x 18in (7 x 44cm)
8. 18 x 3¾in (44 x 9cm)
11. 3 x 18in (7 x 44cm)
6. 4 x 12½in (10 x 30cm)
4. 12 x 3½in (28 x 8cm)
7. 4 x 12½in (10 x 30cm)
2. 3½ x 7½in (8 x 18cm)
1. 7 x 7½in (16 x 18cm)
3. 3½ x 7½in (8 x 18cm)
5. 12 x 3½in (28 x 8cm)
9. 4 x 12½in (44 x 9cm)
13. 22 x 3in (54 x 7cm)

Pull Up A Pouffe

This is a fun and easy project to make and a great way to use scraps of upholstery fabric or thicker fabrics, such as wool or velvet. You can definitely make one of these in an afternoon— just in time for a party or gathering when you need extra seating. It also makes a great present, as you can create something unique and personal as well as incredibly useful.

Depending on the fabric you use, this pouffe can be made for kids, teens, or adults. You could make a couple for your children's rooms out of vintage floral bark cloth, or create something more contemporary from old Welsh blankets for your living room.

The design

For this pouffe, I wanted to use a special piece of 1930s floral upholstery fabric. The colors were so cheery that I thought it would be great for one of the kids' rooms. I also had an old Indian kantha quilt that was torn in places—too much to mend—so, I cut it up. Yes, I cut it into pieces. If I hadn't, it would still be in the cupboard, never to see the light of day. To complete the selection, I added in some sturdy block-printed cottons.

Piecing it together

Gather up the fabrics that you want to use and think about how they will work together. What colors and patterns do you want to sit next to each other? Line them up, so you can see how the finished pouffe will look.

Cutting out

Draw up the paper patterns by following the diagrams on page 86. Cut out the pattern pieces and stick together the two long panels at side A, matching the lines of xxxxx. All seam allowances are ½in (1cm) and are included in the measurements given.

Using the paper patterns, cut 16 of the long panel and two of the top panel, making sure you transfer the dots and crosses, too.

Note: If your fabric isn't long enough, you can use the pattern pieces individually and sew the fabric together at the seam marked xxxxx using a ½in (1cm) seam allowance to get the correct length.

Finished size

Height 12½in (32cm); diameter 26in (66cm).

Note: Metric to imperial conversions are calculated to increments not less than ¼in. Please work consistently in one system (metric) or the other (imperial).

Pouffe cover

It is better to use upholstery-weight fabrics for this project, as lighter cottons will tear after constant use. You will need approximately 2¼–2¾yd (2–2.5m) of fabric, depending on the fabric width. Upholstery fabric and wool cloth are often wider than dressmaking fabric. If you are using lots of different pieces of fabric, make sure they are at least 20in (50cm) in length.

You'll also need

Stuffing—you have several options: leftover fabric scraps, feathers, polyester stuffing, or beanbag filling. Each has its own advantages and disadvantages. You will need a lot of feathers or fabric scraps to fill a pouffe, but you may have a stash that needs using up. Both of these will make the pouffe quite heavy, so polyester or beanbag filling could be better choices if the pouffe is for small children, as they will be able to move it around themselves.

Sewing thread—100 percent cotton all-purpose thread in a neutral color.

Embroidery silk in a color of your choice.

Paper to draw up the pattern.

Sewing the pieces together

With right sides facing, pin and sew together two of the long panels at side B. Repeat this until you have eight pieces. Press the seams open (a steam iron will give the best results on heavier fabric).

Take two of the eight panels and pin them together along sides C and D, with right sides facing. Sew them together, making sure you pivot at each dot. Press the seams open, taking care to really get into the corners to make them sharp.

Repeat this with another two panels. Then join these two sections together. You have now made half of the pouffe cover.

Repeat this process for the other four panels. Now you have two halves.

Pin the two halves with right sides together, but leave a gap approximately 12in (30cm) long on one of the edges. This is so you can stuff the pouffe. Sew together, making sure you pivot at the dots. Press your last seams.

Finishing the pouffe

Turn the cover right side out and stuff the pouffe with your chosen filling until it is as firm as you want. Pin the opening together, with the raw edges turned in, and use a needle and thread to close it with slipstitch.

Fold and press the edges of your top panels ½in (1cm) to the wrong side, so that you have a smaller hexagonal top with no raw edges showing.

Take one hexagonal panel and pin it, wrong side down, to the center of the pouffe (where all the seams have joined). Take care to line up the edges to the lines of each section. Sew the top panel to your pouffe using the embroidery thread. I used a simple slipstitch, but you could use a blanket stitch or any other decorative stitch.

Repeat this for the bottom of the pouffe, and you are done.

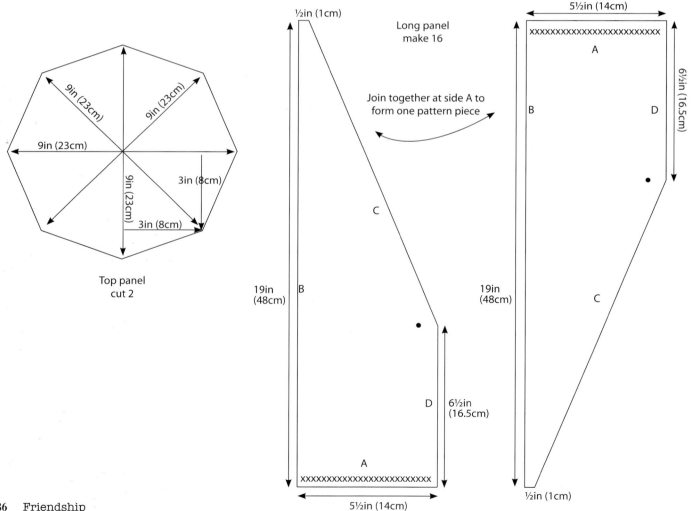

Top panel
cut 2

Long panel
make 16

Join together at side A to form one pattern piece

Backyard Picnic Quilt

A picnic is a marvelous thing. It means summer days and blissful surroundings. It is also likely to involve delicious food and wine—perhaps a barbecue, but most definitely a selection of fantastic treats made specially for the occasion. And, of course, it means people—family and friends gathering together, possibly for a celebration, but maybe just to bask in the summer sun. There will be children running and playing, games being invented, and different generations sharing stories, music, and laughter. These halcyon days are often too rare, but always remembered.

A quilt can anchor you all—providing a place to sit, to lie, to stretch out your legs; a keeper of summer memories, it can be somewhere to lay out the food or to let the baby rest. At the end of the day, shake it out, fold it up and pack it away with the bliss of the occasion wrapped inside it.

The design

A picnic quilt needs to be robust. It has to withstand food, dogs, and children, not to mention sudden changes in the weather. It shouldn't be precious, but should be something that handles the onset of age well. It needs to be a big, bold design that is also simple to make.

This design, essentially made up of six large blocks, is a playful cross between a road map and a table setting. I thought it would be fun for kids to play on—think of the games they could come up with—and also provide an entertaining way to lay out your food. Or, I guess, you could just sit on it.

For me, there was only one choice of fabric for this quilt—Gambian cottons. All the fabric is hand-dyed, using a combination of stitching and wax-stamping to create a resist before hand-dyeing in kola nut and indigo. These simple graphic designs have a fantastic naïve feel that I love. The dark browns and indigos look wonderful nestled against grass and ground and leaves.

Because these fabrics were so bold, I used a cotton canvas as a strong contrast for the borders, as well as for the backing and binding.

Finished size
The finished quilt measures 84 x 84in (210 x 210cm), so it will accommodate lots of people, food, and games.

Quilt top
For this quilt I would use cotton only and make triply sure that you wash and press everything before you begin. You will need at least 2¼yd (2.2m) of fabric for your borders and approximately 3¼yd (3m) of fabric for the individual centers. It is up to you how many different fabrics you use for these, as the border fabric can be used to hold the design together. You might have a collection of 1950s tablecloths, which would be fun, or lots of 1930s floral fabrics, which look gorgeous. Choose the border fabric last, so that you can find something to meld your centers together.

Quilt backing
You will need approximately 5yd (4.5m) of backing fabric, depending on the fabric width. Just make sure that you choose something that won't mind being in contact with the ground—an old blanket would be great (and then you won't need to use any batting), or a light denim or waxed cotton would also be perfect.

Quilt binding
You will need approximately ½yd (0.5m) of fabric. Again, you can use your leftovers or introduce another fabric.

You'll also need
Batting—a piece approximately 4in (10cm) larger all round than the quilt top. Skip this if you are using a blanket for the backing.

Sewing thread—100 percent cotton all-purpose thread in a neutral color.

Quilting thread—100 percent cotton in a color of your choice.

The canvas is sturdy and machine-washable, and, with the Gambian fabrics all pre-washed, this is a quilt that will keep on going for many picnics to come.

Piecing it together

This quilt is made up of six large blocks, plus the borders, and is incredibly simple to make.

Preparing the border fabric

The first place to start is with your border fabric. To do it the quick way, cut or tear 5in (12cm) strips all the way down the length of the fabric. The longest piece you will need is 85in (212cm), so make sure your fabric is at least this long. Once you have done this, set five of these strips aside for the outside and middle borders. Then press the rest and place them in a pile.

If you prefer, you can cut the strips of border fabric to the exact lengths specified on the diagram on page 92, rather than sewing long strips and trimming the excess. It will take you longer to make, but it is up to you. All seam allowances are ½in (1cm) and are included in the measurements given.

Preparing the centers

Now you need to decide which fabrics are going where in your centers. The easiest way to do this is to trace the diagram on page 92 and draw in where each fabric will go. If you have any small pieces of fabric, position them first. Once you have an arrangement you are happy with, you can cut all the pieces.

Cut the pieces block by block and stack them into block piles with number 1 at the top (pencil the number on the back of each piece if it helps). You should end up with six different piles, plus a pile of border fabric.

Building the blocks

Begin piecing the blocks together, starting with block A and using the diagram on page 92 as a guide. With right sides together, pin and sew AC1 to a long strip of the border fabric (AB1). Then trim off the excess border fabric. Press the seams. Keep using the same border strip until it is not long enough to match a center piece, then put it aside and pick up a new strip.

With right sides together, as before, pin and sew AC2 to the strip of border fabric (AB2). Trim off any excess border

fabric. Then pin and sew AC3 to the other side of this piece. Press the seams. Join this block to the first block, and press.

Pin and sew AC4 to a strip of border fabric (AB3). Trim off the excess. Press the seams and then join this to the previous block. Press the seams.

To finish block A, pin and sew a strip of border fabric (AB4) across the bottom of the block. Trim off any excess and press.

Your first block is complete. Repeat this process for the remaining five blocks (B–F).

Joining the blocks together

When all six blocks are complete, the next step is to join them together. With right sides facing, pin and sew block A to block B. Then add block C to this. In the same way, pin and sew block E to block F. Then add block D to this. Press all the seams.

Take one of the five border strips that you set aside and use this as the central piece GB1. With right sides together, pin and sew this to block A/B/C, then pin and sew the other edge to block D/E/F. Trim the excess from GB1 and press all the seams.

Add the four outer border strips, GB2, GB3, GB4, and GB5, following the diagram. Press the seams and trim the excess border fabric as you go. Your quilt top is complete.

Making the quilt

First make your backing. Sew your chosen pieces together until you have a square at least 92 x 92in (230 x 230cm).

Then make the quilt sandwich, following the instructions on page 128. Note: If you decide to use a blanket as the backing, you will not need to use batting as well. You will only need to join the quilt top to the blanket backing.

Machine- or hand-quilt the sandwich. The different options are explained on page 131. I hand-quilted this design, by quilting ¼in (5mm) away from the seam line of each square using a simple running stitch.

Trim your quilt so that the edges are even. This makes attaching the binding much easier. Make and attach the binding, following the instructions on pages 132–3.

Check the weather, plan your picnic, gather your family and friends, and let the fun begin.

Finished size when trimmed and bound: 84 x 84in (210 x 210cm)

Note: Metric to imperial conversions are calculated to increments not less than ¼in. Please work consistently in one system (metric) or the other (imperial).

GB4. 5 x 85in (12 x 212cm)

GB2. 77 x 5in (192 x 12cm)

GB5. 5 x 85in (12 x 212cm)

AC1. 9 x 29in (22 x 72cm)

AB1. 5 x 29in (12 x 72cm)

AC2. 13 x 13in (32 x 32cm)

AB2. 13 x 5in (32 x 12cm)

AC3. 13 x 13in (32 x 32cm)

AB3. 5 x 29in (12 x 72cm)

AC4. 9 x 29in (22 x 72cm)

GB1. 5 x 77in (12 x 192cm)

DC1. 17 x 17in (42 x 42cm)

DB1. 5 x 17in (12 x 42cm)

DC2. 9 x 17in (22 x 42cm)

DB2. 5 x 17in (12 x 42cm)

DC3. 5 x 17in (12 x 42cm)

DB3. 37 x 5in (92 x 12cm)

EC1. 9 x 21in (22 x 52cm)

EB1. 5 x 21in (12 x 52cm)

EC2. 7 x 5in (17 x 12cm)

EB2. 7 x 5in (17 x 12cm)

EC3. 7 x 12in (17 x 32cm)

EB4. 5 x 43in (12 x 107cm)

FC1. 15 x 17in (37 x 42cm)

AB4. 37 x 5in (92 x 12cm)

BC1. 13 x 9in (32 x 22cm)

BB2. 5 x 29in (12 x 72cm)

BC3. 21 x 17in (52 x 42cm)

BB1. 13 x 5in (32 x 12cm)

BC2. 13 x 17in (32 x 42cm)

BB3. 21 x 5in (52 x 12cm)

BC4. 21 x 9in (52 x 22cm)

EB3. 19 x 5in (47 x 12cm)

EC4. 19 x 19in (47 x 47cm)

FB1. 15 x 5in (37 x 12cm)

FC2. 15 x 17in (37 x 42cm)

FB2. 15 x 5in (37 x 12cm)

CB1. 37 x 5in (92 x 12cm)

CC1. 21 x 13in (52 x 32cm)

CB2. 5 x 13in (12 x 32cm)

CC2. 13 x 13in (32 x 32cm)

EB5. 23 x 5in (57 x 12cm)

EC5. 23 x 11in (57 x 27cm)

FB3. 5 x 17in (12 x 42cm)

FC3. 11 x 17in (27 x 42cm)

GB3. 77 x 5in (192 x 12cm)

Memories

All memories, happy or sad, are deeply personal. There are places and experiences that move us and stay with us. There are special things we collect, which may have no practical use but still mean the world to us—a scrap of lace, a child's dress, or a handkerchief can all evoke powerful emotions. Then there are people—those we know now or those we have left behind or lost forever. People who have played a starring role in our lives and the walk-ons. The thread that binds all these memories together can take us back years in a second. Why not let all of them take you forward? Stitch and bind them into your future instead.

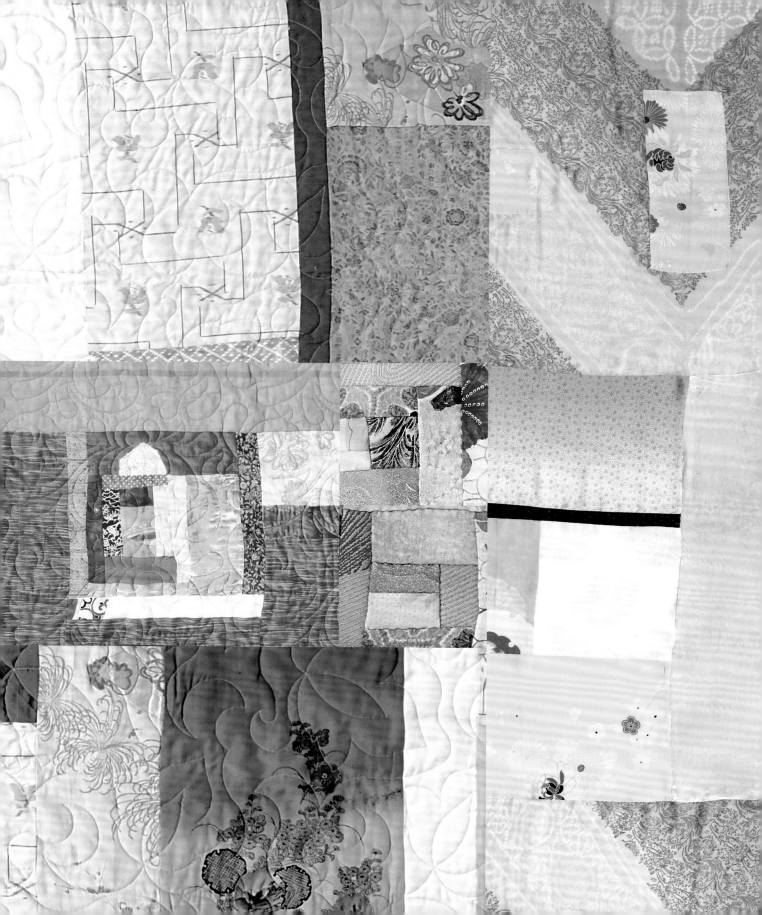

Celebration Of Life Quilt

The poet Robert Frost wrote about choosing the road less traveled—making your own path through life. I read that poem when I was 15 and it has been my traveling companion ever since. I have made some good and some not so good decisions, but I hope that when I get to the end of my life, I can look back at my twisty, windy journey and feel pretty proud of the road I chose.

This quilt is about your life, your road, and the important stops you made on the way. Some are more life changing than others, but many deserve acknowledgment. This is a quilt you can make now, or one that you can spend years making. It can also be one that you make for someone you love—a person who has lived a remarkable life.

The design

This quilt is made up of three parts—the road and paths, the stops (patches), and the support surrounding them. The road leading you through the quilt is, of course, a little off-center. The paths vary in distance and the stops are different sizes, because life is like that, isn't it?

Although it looks complicated to make, I promise you it is not—it is built on the same principle as most quilts, in that you are simply building blocks. The hardest part will be choosing the fabric, as this is probably the most personal quilt you can make.

I had recently dyed a batch of silk velvet using natural dyes and this became the basis of my color palette. By dipping the velvet continually into the same pot of dye, the finished result was everything from the palest dusky pink to a rich, dark mulberry—just lovely. I mixed in all kinds of silks in myriad colors—from pumpkin, to smoky purple, to silver—and a story was created.

For the backing, I used a mixture of dark pink, ivory, and gray/green fine wools. Finally, I bound the quilt with leftover pieces from the top, so that it wouldn't battle with the main design.

Finished size
The finished quilt measures 84 x 84in (210 x 210cm).

Quilt top
You will need approximately 6½yd (6m) of fabric for this design, with a mixture of large and small pieces. You will need the large pieces (approximately 4½yd/4m) for the background fabric and a strip at least 87in (220cm) long for the main road. Apart from this, you can use lots of smaller pieces for the individual patches and it is a perfect opportunity to use really special scraps.

Quilt backing
You will need approximately 5½yd (5m) of backing fabric for this size quilt. The backing can be made up of the leftovers from the quilt top or you can use something new.

Quilt binding
You will need approximately ½yd (0.5m) of fabric. Again, you can use your leftovers or introduce another fabric.

You'll also need
Batting—a piece approximately 4in (10cm) larger all round than the quilt top.

Sewing thread—100 percent cotton all-purpose thread in a neutral color.

Quilting thread—100 percent cotton in a color of your choice.

Tip for sewing silk and velvet
If you are using silks or velvets for this quilt, make sure you use a walking foot and a fine needle on your sewing machine.

Piecing it together

Start by planning your fabrics—decide what you are going to use for the support pieces and where. I have used a mixture of four different fabrics, but you could just use one, and this would make your patches, paths, and road stand out even more. Then think about the road and paths and decide what you want to use for them. Again, you can use one fabric for them all, or a selection. Try to make sure that you have individual pieces that are long enough to use for these. If it helps, you can trace the design from the diagrams on pages 100–102 and plan or color in where each fabric will go.

Cutting out

Following the diagram on pages 102, cut the pieces from your support fabrics. Remember, all seam allowances are ½in (1cm) and are included in the measurements given on the diagram. Pencil the number of each piece on the back, and then group them into each individual block:

A1, A2, A4, A6
B1, B2, B4, B6
C1, C2, C4, C6, C7
D1, D3, D5, D6
E1, E3, E4, E6
F1, F2, F4, F6
G1, G3, G4, G6
H1, H3, H4, H6, H7
I1, I3, I5, I6

Then cut your road and paths—mark the numbers on the back and put them aside or in labeled envelopes:

A5, B5, C5, D4, E2, F3, G2, H2, I2, J

Now cut and sew your patches. By cutting the larger parts of the quilt first, you will have leftover fabric that you may want to incorporate into some or all of your patches. These patches work on the same principle as the Housewarming Pillow (see page 80), so follow those instructions for making them, using the measurements on the diagrams on pages 100–101. Make two of patch A, two of patch B, three of patch C, and two of patch D.

You now have nine patches and all of the required pieces to create your quilt.

Building the blocks

Start by sewing block A, using the main quilt diagram on page 102 as your guide.

With right sides together, pin and sew A2 to a patch A3. Press the seams.

With right sides together, as before, pin and sew A4 to A5, then pin and sew A6 to the other edge of A5. Press the seams.

Pin and sew A2/patch A3 to A4/A5/A6. Press the seams.

Pin and sew this group to A1. Press the seams and your first block is complete.

Repeat this process for the remaining eight blocks.

Joining the blocks together

With right sides together, pin and sew block A to block B. Add block C to this and then block D. Press your seams and set the piece aside.

Pin and sew block E to block F. Continue to add blocks G, H and then I, until this side is complete. Press your seams.

Pin and sew the left-hand edge of piece J to the right-hand edge of block A/B/C/D. Then pin and sew the left-hand edge of block E/F/G/H/I to the remaining edge of piece J. Take care to line up pieces B5 and G2 when you are sewing.

Press your seams and your quilt top is complete.

Making the quilt

First make your backing. Sew your chosen pieces together until you have a square at least 92 x 92in (230 x 230cm) or 4in (10cm) larger all round than your finished quilt top.

Make the quilt sandwich, following the instructions on page 128.

Machine- or hand-quilt the sandwich. The different options are explained on page 131. I chose to have this design long-arm quilted with an elegant feather design. This helps to tie all the pieces together and makes the quilt a little flatter, which I think works for this design.

Trim the quilt so the edges are even. This makes attaching the binding much easier. Make and attach the binding, following the instructions on pages 132–3.

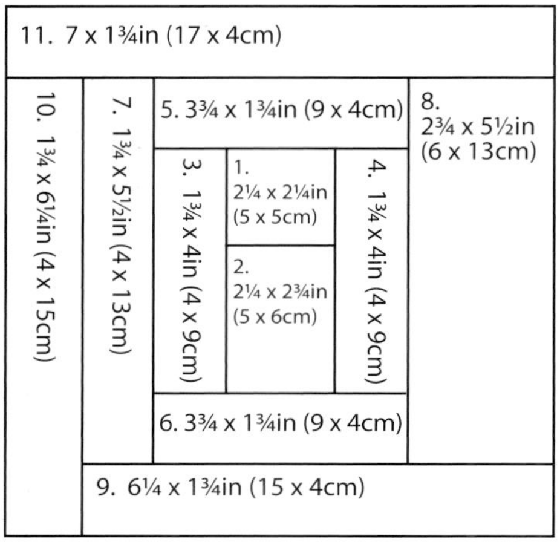

Note: Metric to imperial conversions are calculated to increments not less than ¼in. Please work consistently in one system (metric) or the other (imperial).

Patch A: 6 x 6in (15 x 15cm)
make 2 (A3 and H5)

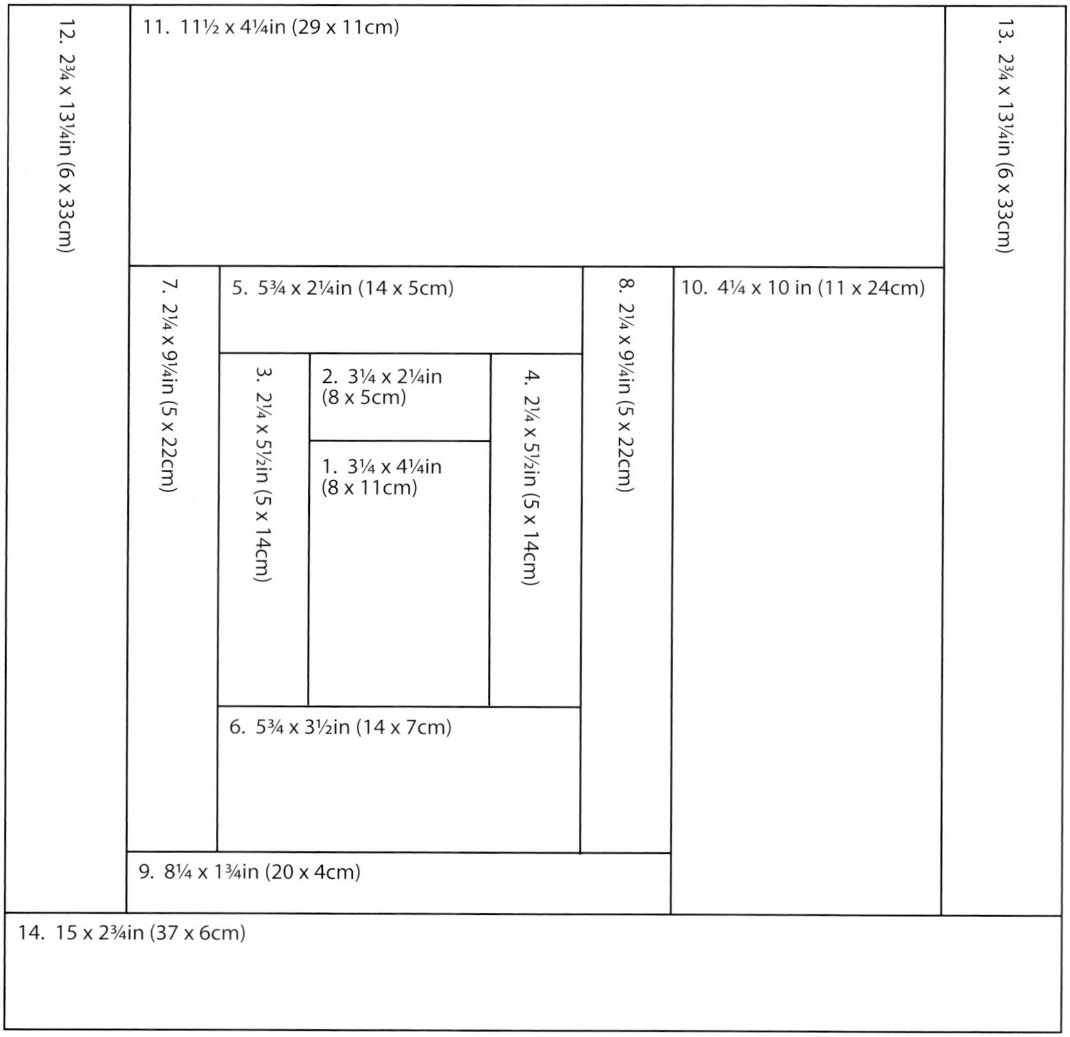

11. 7 x 1¾in (17 x 4cm)

10. 1¾ x 6¼in (4 x 15cm)

7. 1¾ x 5½in (4 x 13cm)

5. 3¾ x 1¾in (9 x 4cm)

8. 2¾ x 5½in (6 x 13cm)

3. 1¾ x 4in (4 x 9cm)

1. 2¼ x 2¼in (5 x 5cm)

2. 2¼ x 2¾in (5 x 6cm)

4. 1¾ x 4in (4 x 9cm)

6. 3¾ x 1¾in (9 x 4cm)

9. 6¼ x 1¾in (15 x 4cm)

Patch B: 14 x 14in (35 x 35cm)
make 2 (D2 and E5)

12. 2¾ x 13¼in (6 x 33cm)

11. 11½ x 4¼in (29 x 11cm)

13. 2¾ x 13¼in (6 x 33cm)

7. 2¼ x 9¼in (5 x 22cm)

5. 5¾ x 2¼in (14 x 5cm)

3. 2¼ x 5½in (5 x 14cm)

2. 3¼ x 2¼in (8 x 5cm)

1. 3¼ x 4¼in (8 x 11cm)

4. 2¼ x 5½in (5 x 14cm)

8. 2¼ x 9¼in (5 x 22cm)

10. 4¼ x 10 in (11 x 24cm)

6. 5¾ x 3½in (14 x 7cm)

9. 8¼ x 1¾in (20 x 4cm)

14. 15 x 2¾in (37 x 6cm)

Patch C: 12 x 12in (30 x 30cm)
make 3 (B3, G5 and I4)

12. 2¼ x 13in (5 x 32cm)

9. 10½ x 2¼in (26 x 5cm)

8. 10½ x 2½in (26 x 6cm)

6. 2½ x 7½in (6 x 18cm)

4. 7½ x 2¼in (18 x 5cm)

7. 2½ x 7½in (6 x 18cm)

2. 3 x 5in (7 x 12cm)

1. 3½ x 5in (8 x 12cm)

3. 3 x 5in (7 x 12cm)

5. 7½ x 2¼in (18 x 5cm)

13. 2¼ x 13in (5 x 32cm)

10. 10½ x 2½in (26 x 6cm)

11. 10½ x 2¼in (26 x 5cm)

Patch D: 10 x 10in (25 x 25cm)
make 2 (C3 and F5)

12. 11 x 2¾in (27 x 7cm)

10. 2¾ x 5¾in (6 x 15cm)

8. 2¼ x 5¾in (5 x 15cm)

7. 4¼ x 1¾in (11 x 4cm)

4. 1¾ x 4¼in (4 x 11cm)

2. 2¾ x 1¾in (7 x 4cm)

1. 2¾ x 2¾in (7 x 7cm)

5. 1¾ x 4¼in (4 x 11cm)

9. 2¼ x 5¾in (5 x 15cm)

11. 3½ x 5¾in (8 x 15cm)

3. 2¾ x 1¾in (7 x 4cm)

6. 4¼ x 1¾in (11 x 4cm)

13. 11 x 4½in (27 x 9cm)

Finished size when trimmed and bound:
84 x 84in (210 x 210cm)

J

A	A1			J1	E1		E4		E6		E
	A2	A4			E2						
		A5			E3			E5			
	A3	A6									
B	B1				F1						F
	B2	B3	B4		F2	F5	F6				
			B5		F3						
			B6		F4						
C	C1				G1		G4		G6		G
	C2	C3	C4		G2						
			C5		G3			G5			
			C6								
	C7				H1		H4	H6			H
D	D1		D3		H2		H5				
		D2	D4		H3						
			D5		H7						
	D6				I1		I4	I5			I
					I2						
					I3						
					I6						

A1. 37 x 11in (92 x 27cm)
A2. 5 x 7in (12 x 17cm)
A3. patch A
A4. 27 x 3in (67 x 7cm)
A5. 27 x 3in (67 x 7cm)
A6. 27 x 3in (67 x 7cm)

B1. 37 x 15in (92 x 37cm)
B2. 17 x 13in (42 x 32cm)
B3. patch C
B4. 9 x 7in (22 x 17cm)
B5. 9 x 3in (22 x 7cm)
B6. 9 x 5in (22 x 12cm)

C1. 37 x 7in (92 x 17cm)
C2. 5 x 11in (12 x 27cm)
C3. patch D
C4. 23 x 7in (57 x 17cm)
C5. 23 x 3in (57 x 7cm)
C6. 23 x 3in (57 x 7cm)
C7. 37 x 7in (92 x 17cm)

D1. 17 x 15in (42 x 37cm)
D2. patch B
D3. 7 x 7in (17 x 17cm)
D4. 7 x 3in (17 x 7cm)
D5. 7 x 7in (17 x 17cm)
D6. 37 x 7in (92 x 17cm)

E1. 21 x 9in (52 x 22cm)
E2. 21 x 3in (52 x 7cm)
E3. 21 x 7in (52 x 17cm)
E4. 15 x 3in (37 x 7cm)
E5. patch B
E6. 11 x 17in (27 x 42cm)

F1. 45 x 5in (112 x 12cm)
F2. 5 x 5in (12 x 12cm)
F3. 5 x 3in (12 x 7cm)
F4. 5 x 5in (12 x 12cm)
F5. patch D
F6. 31 x 11in (77 x 27cm)

G1. 29 x 7in (72 x 17cm)
G2. 29 x 3in (72 x 7cm)
G3. 29 x 7in (72 x 17cm)
G4. 13 x 3in (32 x 7cm)
G5. patch C
G6. 5 x 15in (12 x 37cm)

H1. 17 x 7in (42 x 17cm)
H2. 17 x 3in (42 x 7cm)
H3. 17 x 3in (42 x 7cm)
H4. 7 x 5in (17 x 12cm)
H5. patch A
H6. 23 x 11in (57 x 27cm)
H7. 45 x 11in (112 x 27cm)

I1. 13 x 7in (32 x 17cm)
I2. 13 x 3in (32 x 7cm)
I3. 13 x 5in (32 x 12cm)
I4. patch C
I5. 21 x 13in (52 x 32cm)
I6. 45 x 9in (112 x 22cm)

J. 5 x 85in (12 x 212cm)

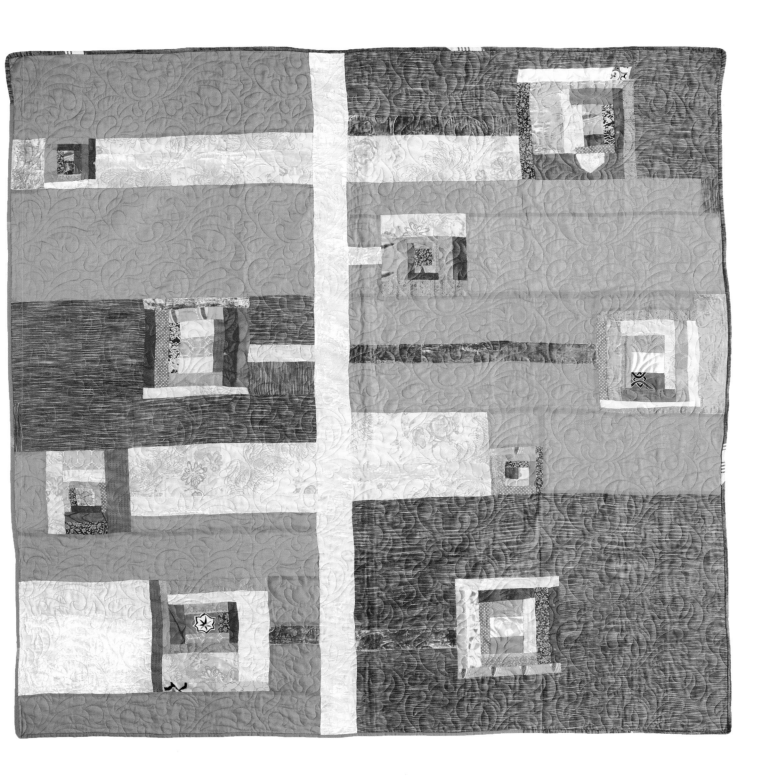

Traveler's Tales Quilt

Traveling around the world is our great opportunity to escape from the day-to-day stuff of life. Whether you are slinging on a backpack for a 12-month sabbatical or jumping onto a budget airline for a fortnight on a Greek island, it gives you the chance to be truly yourself. And you get to see new places and everything else in a completely different way.

Shopping in these far-flung destinations is one of the great pleasures of traveling. Picking out a sari from a market stall in India, a blanket from a roadside seller in Kenya, or scraps of precious antique linen from a brocante in France, cultivates our memories of both the places and the people. Unfortunately, we (and that includes me) often bring our purchases home, put them in a cupboard, and get on with our lives. This is the time to bring those treasures out and turn your adventures, great and small, into a quilt of happy memories.

The design

This quilt started with two pieces of fabric—a bolt of mauve Japanese wool and the butter-colored lining of an antique French jacket. Two very different destinations and design sensibilities, but both fabrics have charming details. I added a lilac-and-gray sari and some smoky-purple silk from the East, and this combination formed the basis of a very gentle and grown-up quilt. Although I mixed together silk, cotton, and wool here, I made sure that the fabric weights were pretty equal. I wanted the backing to be simple, so I used a hand-loomed ivory cotton from India, and bound the quilt in gray habotai silk.

Tip for fabric shopping

If you need to shop for additional fabric to go with your traveler's stash, take a snip of each of the fabrics you are using with you. This avoids toting a heavy bag around but also lets you find other pieces that work with what you have without relying on memory alone.

Finished size
The finished quilt measures 84 x 88in (210 x 220cm).

Quilt top
It is difficult to prescribe an exact amount of fabric, but you will need at least 5½yd (5m).

Lay out all of the fabric that you want to use to give you a clear idea of how much you have. If you don't have enough, head to a fabric store or a market to fill in the gaps. If you are lucky enough to have too much fabric (those saris are hard to resist), it is a matter of editing it down.

Find combinations that are pleasing to you. Each piece could be a unique fabric, or you might prefer to repeat fabrics throughout the quilt—it's up to you. There are varying sizes in this design, so precious embroideries can be balanced with larger, simpler pieces. If you have any special small pieces, plan them first.

Quilt backing
You will need around 5½yd (5m) of backing fabric for the full-size quilt. A whole sari would be ideal, as would an old French linen sheet or a couple of Balinese sarongs. Otherwise, you could use leftovers from the front or find something completely new/old.

Quilt binding
You will need approximately ½yd (0.5m) of fabric. Again, you can use your leftovers or introduce another fabric.

You'll also need
Batting—a piece approximately 4in (10cm) larger all round than the quilt top.

Sewing thread—100 percent cotton all-purpose thread in a neutral color.

Quilting thread—100 percent cotton in a color of your choice.

The design is based on a Korean Pojagi quilt that I saw many years ago. The pattern seems random, but it isn't really—there are just lots of different-size pieces so that you can accommodate both the saris and the smaller scraps. The quilt is divided into three sections, or blocks, so you can make one, two, or all three. The full-size quilt is for a queen-size bed; two sections would make a great throw for the end of the bed; while one section would form a lovely blanket for the sofa. It all depends on your travels and your patience.

Piecing it together

There are two ways to build this quilt, depending on how confident you are in visualizing fabric combinations. If you are not confident, don't be alarmed: it can be hard to do and, as these pieces are quite large, it is better to be safe than to cut your fabric incorrectly.

The first way to build the quilt is to do it one block at a time. That is, plan and then cut A, B, or C—just concentrating on those 15–18 pieces (see the diagram on page 108). Once you have cut and pieced the first block, then you can move on to the next one.

The second way is to cut the quilt as one big block. You will have to make more decisions initially, but you will have slightly more control over the overall flow of the quilt.

Either way, you will sew the quilt block by block.

Trace the diagram on page 108 and use coloring pencils to plan your design.

Cutting out

Make sure you have enough space to lay everything out— a bed, the floor, or a wall to pin everything on all work well. From your pile of fabrics, start placing pieces next to each other to get combinations that you like. Then, following the diagram on page 108, cut the pieces to the required size. All seam allowances are ½in (1cm) and are included in the measurements given on the diagram.

You don't have to start with A1. I often choose and cut the largest pieces first, to make sure that I have big enough pieces available for these. Don't forget to maximize those small precious pieces, too. Mark each piece number on the back with a pencil as you work.

When you have cut a complete block, or the whole quilt, you can start sewing it together.

Building the blocks

As with the other quilts in the book, you are just trying to build blocks, so that you are only sewing straight lines and not around corners. So, starting with block A, pin and sew A1 to A2, with right sides facing. Press the seams. Then add A3 to this—pin, sew, and press. Then add A4—pin, sew, and press. This completes a block within a block.

Looking at the diagram, you can see that you then join A5 to A6, and then add A7 to those two. Then you join this mini block to the first block you have made.

Continue building up block A in this way. Once you have got the hang of this method, the quilt is satisfyingly speedy to make.

When you have finished block A, move on to block B and then block C.

Joining the blocks

When you have completed all three blocks, simply sew them together, with right sides facing, along the long edges. There are a few points in the quilt where seam lines do match up between blocks, so make sure you match and pin these before you sew. Press the seams, and your quilt top is complete.

Making the quilt

First make the backing. Sew your chosen pieces together until you have a square at least 92 x 96in (230 x 240cm) or 4in (10cm) larger all round than your finished quilt top.

Make the quilt sandwich, following the instructions on page 128.

Machine- or hand-quilt the sandwich. The different options are explained on page 131. I had this quilt long-arm quilted, as I wanted it to have a sophisticated feel.

Trim the quilt so that the edges are even. This makes attaching the binding much easier. Make and attach the binding, following the instructions on pages 132–3.

I promise you that every time you see this quilt, you will remember your favorite oceans, mountains, cities, or people from all your travels—it is a truly wonderful feeling.

Finished size when trimmed and bound: 84 x 88in (210 x 220cm)

Note: Metric to imperial conversions are calculated to increments not less than ¼in.
Please work consistently in one system (metric) or the other (imperial).

Section A
- A14. 5 x 29in (12 x 72cm)
- A1. 7 x 13in (17 x 32cm)
- A2. 33 x 13in (82 x 32cm)
- A3. 7 x 13in (17 x 32cm)
- A4. 7 x 32cm (3 x 13in)
- A8. 11 x 29in (27 x 72cm)
- A9. 7 x 17in (17 x 42cm)
- A11. 13 x 29in (32 x 72cm)
- A12. 3 x 29in (7 x 72cm)
- A13. 5 x 29in (12 x 72cm)
- A5. 35 x 13in (87 x 32cm)
- A7. 13 x 17in (32 x 42cm)
- A10. 7 x 13in (17 x 32cm)
- A6. 35 x 5in (87 x 12cm)

Section B
- B1. 5 x 21in (12 x 52cm)
- B3. 13 x 13in (32 x 32cm)
- B5. 7 x 33in (17 x 82cm)
- B6. 6 x 5in (17 x 12cm)
- B8. 9 x 25in (22 x 62cm)
- B7. 7 x 29in (17 x 72cm)
- B10. 13 x 13in (32 x 32cm)
- B12. 7 x 33in (17 x 82cm)
- B13. 13 x 21in (32 x 52cm)
- B15. 3 x 33in (7 x 82cm)
- B16. 13 x 9in (32 x 22cm)
- B19. 5 x 33in (12 x 82cm)
- B4. 13 x 21in (32 x 52cm)
- B11. 13 x 21in (32 x 52cm)
- B17. 13 x 17in (32 x 42cm)
- B14. 13 x 13in (32 x 32cm)
- B9. 9 x 9in (22 x 22cm)
- B18. 13 x 9in (32 x 22cm)
- B2. 5 x 13in (12 x 32cm)

Section C
- C1. 7 x 29in (17 x 72cm)
- C2. 3 x 29in (7 x 72cm)
- C3. 9 x 29in (22 x 72cm)
- C4. 13 x 13in (32 x 32cm)
- C6. 7 x 9in (17 x 22cm)
- C8. 13 x 7in (32 x 17cm)
- C11. 7 x 23in (17 x 57cm)
- C12. 13 x 17in (32 x 42cm)
- C14. 5 x 23in (12 x 57cm)
- C15. 13 x 7in (32 x 17cm)
- C18. 5 x 29in (12 x 72cm)
- C9. 13 x 21in (32 x 52cm)
- C16. 13 x 17in (32 x 42cm)
- C7. 7 x 21in (17 x 52cm)
- C5. 13 x 17in (32 x 42cm)
- C13. 13 x 7in (32 x 17cm)
- C17. 35 x 7in (87 x 17cm)
- C10. 13 x 3in (32 x 7cm)

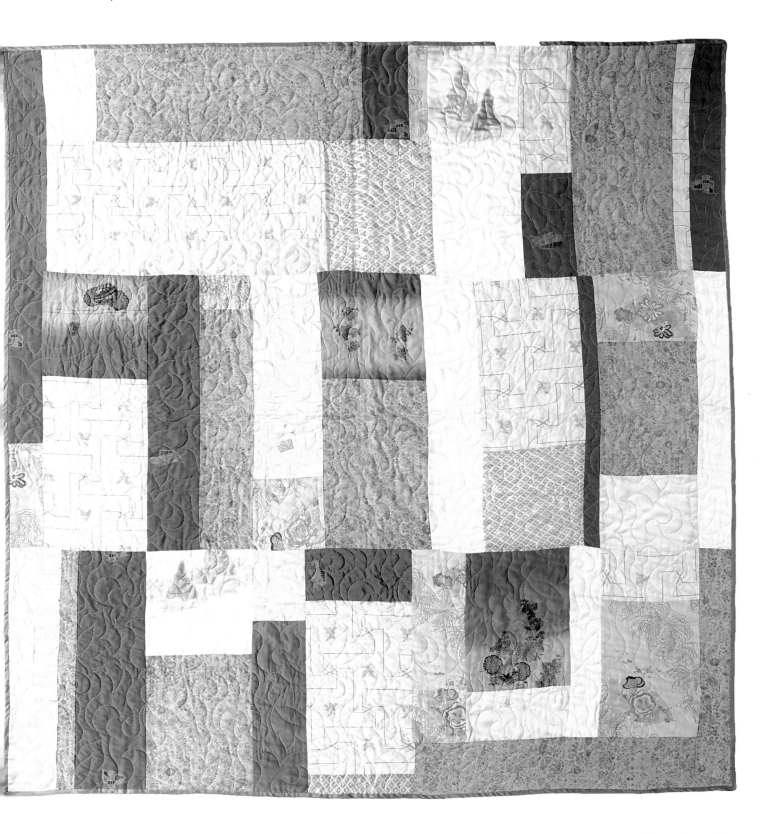

Keepsake Artworks

When people we love pass away, all we have left are their possessions. Their clothes often stay with us and we know not what to do with them. It seems wrong to send them away, but equally difficult to keep them.

Each of us is remembered for certain pieces of clothing and ways of dressing. They seem to sum us up and be a visual manifestation of who people think we are. I wanted to create something that enables you to keep a piece of somebody close to you. You may like to make more than one, as gifts for family or friends, or you could gather together to make them, so that you can all celebrate the life of someone special.

No doubt these will be deeply personal pieces to make. Hopefully the process of selecting different items and stitching them together will help you, as well as creating tangible and beautiful reminders of someone you loved.

The design

This is piecing at its very simplest—you are completely freestyling. I hand-stitched each of these artworks, as they are only around 8 x 8in (20 x 20cm) in size.

Piecing it together

Gather together the precious pieces of cloth that you would like to use. Then simply cut pieces of fabric as you wish and stitch them together, building the design instinctively as you go and pressing the seams after each addition. My first piece was 2 x 1½in (5 x 4cm) and I then cut a strip approximately 2 x 1in (5 x 2cm) to add to the first piece.

Stitch the first two pieces of fabric together with right sides facing, and press. Choose and cut a third piece of

Finished size
Approximately 8 x 8in (20 x 20cm), but you can make these any size.

You will need
Pieces of cloth that are important to you.

Sewing thread—100 percent cotton all-purpose thread in a neutral color.

Embellishments, such as lace or embroidery thread, if you desire.

Suitable picture frame (these are from Ikea).

fabric and add it to the first two. You can add pieces that are longer and then trim the fabric after you have pressed it. Pieces can be skinny, fat, triangular, or rectangular. Keep turning and adding fabric until your piece is the size you would like. Look at the examples opposite to see how I pieced blocks together. When you are satisfied with your piece, press it carefully.

If you wish, stitch on additional embellishments, such as pretty buttons, pieces of lace, decorative beads, sequins, or embroidery.

Finally, find a frame that suits the piece you have made and the personality of the person for whom you have made it.

Mementos Curtain Panel

I have always had a passion for fine silks and old but beautifully crafted passementerie, and I have envelopes and boxes full of gorgeous scraps. Dusty lace from a French brocante and fine strips of coffee-colored ribbon from the back room of a second-hand store have both found their way home with me. As have Victorian velvet jackets and delicate silk slips from the 1930s, my favorite era for fashion and a great source of inspiration.

Sometimes, I think it is good to make something that is purely beautiful and not at all useful. Beauty lifts the spirit and fills the heart, and often that is more than enough. If you are a fabric lover, you may have cloth that is too fine to turn into a practical quilt but that is ideal to make into a stitched curtain panel—a piece that diffuses the light and gives you joy every time you catch a glimpse of it.

The design

A few years ago I went to an exhibition on French fashion designer Madeleine Vionnet. I could not believe how extraordinary her work was and the exhibition is now a constant reference point for me. Her designs and construction were so mathematical, yet the garments seemed to be free—fine and delicate but with precise and noticeable stitching. The simple shapes and astonishing embroidery created garments of extraordinary beauty. Math, fabric, and intricate stitching are like design nirvana for me.

This curtain panel is based on the same freestyling principle as the "I Love You Quilted Throw" (see page 48)—that is, you build blocks in the same way as for all other quilts, but with no predetermined pattern. If you prefer to plan your panel a little more methodically, rather than freestyling, see page 134, where I have explained how to design your own pattern.

The color palette came from the room in which the curtain is hanging, the small library in our old home, where I spent many hours reading. It was my favorite room and housed my most precious furniture, art, and books.

Finished size

There is no fixed size for this curtain panel—it totally depends on the dimensions of the window or door where it is going to hang. The design will work equally well for a little café-style window or a big set of French doors, so decide where your curtain is for, take the measurements, and then work out the size the curtain needs to be before you begin.

Make the finished width of the curtain between one and a half and two times the width of the window or door, depending on the fullness you want. I prefer the curtain panel to be quite flat, but it is up to you. For the length, I like it to pool slightly, but you may want it to finish exactly at the floor.

Curtain panel

This is a tricky design to give exact fabric quantities for, as it depends on the size you want to make and the fabric you have.

You need to plan your panel in three parts: one solid piece for the top third, a medley of fabrics for the middle, and a second solid piece for the bottom third. By "solid," I mean one single piece of fabric—this is the perfect project to use lace or any other transparent fabric.

You will also need extra fabric for the boro applied pieces (see page 115).

You'll also need

Sewing thread—100 percent cotton all-purpose thread in a neutral color.

Quilting or embroidery thread in a color of your choice.

Some of the fabric I had, some I gathered, ending up with a wonderful combination of an old silk chiffon sari, some kimono silk scraps, the lining from the sleeve of a coat, and some velvet that I over-dyed to achieve the exact color I wanted. That might sound a little pedantic, but I know that I will take this curtain panel with me wherever I go.

Piecing it together

To start, work out the width and length of your curtain panel (see Finished Size, page 112). I made mine so that it pools on the floor, which makes it versatile for future moves, but you may prefer to make it shorter.

Cutting out

Divide the panel into thirds to give you the dimensions for your two solid pieces at the top and bottom of the curtain. Don't forget to add seam allowances to this measurement—I used a seam allowance of ½in (1cm), although you can use a narrower allowance for this project. Cut out the top and bottom pieces and set them aside.

The middle section is where you get to play and piece fabrics to your own design. Pull out all your selected cloth and lay it out on a clear space. Keep moving things around until you have a layout you are really happy with. Build in large and small pieces and don't be afraid of layering fabrics if you like that effect. You might want to draw this section up on graph paper, as explained on page 134. In this case, cut everything to fit, not forgetting your seam allowances.

Sewing the pieces together

Once you have everything planned and laid out, it is time to start sewing. Start from one edge of your panel and work across or down—this makes it easier to manage and to concentrate on.

If you are working with very fine fabric, make sure that you have the right needle on your sewing machine. You may find that changing to a walking foot, if your machine has one, also makes it easier to sew. If your machine doesn't have one, a walking foot is a good investment, as you can use it for sewing fine or slippery fabrics as well as for quilting.

Pin and sew two pieces together with right sides facing. Press the seams, taking care to check that the iron is the correct temperature for the type of fabric you are using. If you haven't pre-planned the size of each piece, you will need to trim off any excess before you join the next piece. Continue cutting and joining pieces, following your layout.

If you find it easier, you can make up several blocks that you then join together into one large panel.

You may find that you need to add extra pieces or subtract pieces from your original layout—just take your time and remember that the principle of building blocks is exactly the same, whether you have a precise pattern or you are creating your own.

Once you have reached the required size, trim off any excess and make sure the four edges of your panel are "square."

Making the curtain panel

With the pieced panel in the center, pin and sew the three sections together with right sides facing. Press the seams.

Turn in the seam allowance around the edge of the curtain panel and sew it in place by hand or machine. Initially, I stitched mine by machine, but after the photograph was taken I decided to unpick it and hand-sew it with an antique metallic thread. Now I feel that I have honored Madame Vionnet's spirit of making.

The boro technique

The last step is to decide whether you would like to apply any patches to your curtain panel. I am really inspired by Japanese boro-style quilts and I thought it would be lovely to use this technique, but with transparent fabrics and fine silks rather than utilitarian cottons.

I simply cut rectangles and placed them in a pleasing pattern. I then pinned and hand-stitched them to the panel with metallic thread, leaving the edges raw. You can do as little or as much of this technique as you want and you can place the patches anywhere you like—perhaps over a damaged piece, or to highlight a particular fabric.

Your panel is complete—I know it will be gorgeous.

I love the true tradition of *quilting*—making fabric that you have and love into *something* that is both useful and beautiful, using your creative eye and your *choices*.

Practicalities

Whether you are baking, sewing, gilding, or quilting, there are certain practicalities, tools, and techniques that you need to know before you get started. As far as quilting goes, once you know the basics, you can choose how you make your quilts. Some traditional quilters insist on one "correct" way to do things. You will also find books that give very long and strict instructions, which make you want to give up before you begin. I definitely don't want that. In the same way as we adjust recipes to suit our personal taste, I want you to find your own way to create quilts.

Technology has given us some great quilting tools that simplify the process and leave us more time to create. I would be lost without a rotary cutter and can't imagine making anything without my sewing machine.

So, this section is all about helping you gather the tools you need and find out how a quilt is put together. Then you can make a quilt that you love in your own special way.

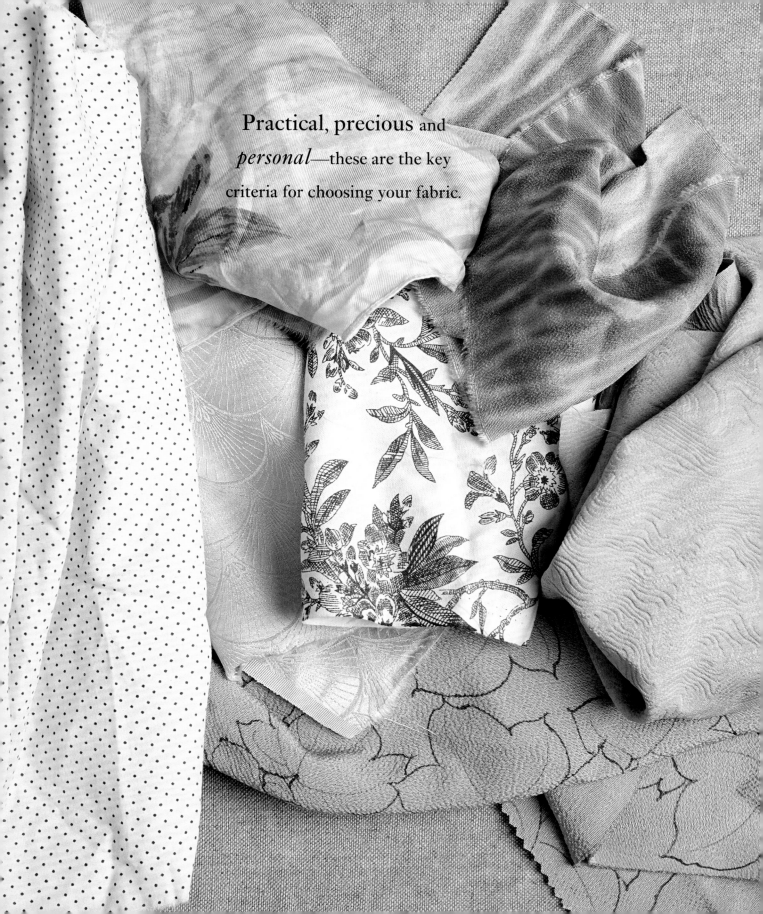

Practical, precious and *personal*—these are the key criteria for choosing your fabric.

Fabric

This is where it all starts—the kimono from an antique's fair, a bolt of wax print from a vacation trip, or even the drawer full of fabric collected over the years. We are drawn to fabric in a way that is more than just visual: fabric can also be a tactile memory of a place or a person.

When you make a quilt, you can mix old and contemporary fabrics, stashes and new purchases, vintage clothes and modern fat quarters. As much as I love sets of fat quarters, I am more inspired by curating my own collection of cloth, because then it truly reflects me. A quilt made from fabric that you love or that holds special memories feels greater than just the quilt itself.

I believe a quilt should be practical—you want to be able to sleep under it or wrap it around you to keep you warm. I think it should also be very personal. No one has had the life you have, so by putting your story, memories, and fabric into a quilt, you make it into something that is also very precious.

Choosing fabrics
You can use most (not all) fabrics in a quilt. The vast majority of fabric used is cotton and, in an ideal world, this is best—it is robust, it doesn't stretch, and it sews together beautifully. However, you may have a passion for vintage silk scarves or antique French linen sheets. You might have your child's baby pajamas or a swatch of your mother's lace wedding dress. Use them—just be aware of the following:

- If you want to use different weights of fabric in a quilt, try and join like to like. If you put a piece of wool against a piece of fine silk, they will have a little tussle and it is likely that the silk will tear. But if you plan the silk to be stitched to a piece of cotton and then the wool, all the fabrics will behave better.

- Different fabrics will perform differently in the long term. Anything very old or handmade will not be as enduring as commercial quilting cotton. But you can always repair, patch or enjoy the process of it wearing and changing.

- Some fabrics won't be practical for some quilts. A quilt for a baby needs to be made out of something fit for the purpose, for obvious reasons. One for a teenage boy or dog needs to be very practical. If the quilt is for you, and it is not going to get a lot of wear and tear, then use whatever you want.

- Silk can be fragile and it will fade in sunlight. I love this aspect of it, but you might not. Very old silk may rip or disintegrate when you quilt it, so you could just use it for tiny patches.

- Lace or chiffon will need to be backed with another fabric before use in a quilt, both so that you don't see the batting beneath it and to give it the additional strength it needs.

- Men's ties are difficult to use in quilt tops, but they could be used for binding because they are cut on the bias.

- Anything knit is complicated because it stretches and can distort the quilt. However, if you iron some interfacing onto the back of it before you cut it, it will behave much better.

- Jeans or thick denim are almost too hard to hand-quilt, but a good long-arm quilter will take on the challenge.

- Antique linen sheets make practical and beautiful backing.

- All cottons are not equal in quality. Hand-loomed cotton from India will be different to Liberty cotton, but both look lovely.

- Man-made fabrics, such as polyester, aren't great in a quilt. They behave differently from natural-fiber cloths when they are washed and sewn, and they are not as tactile or warm.

Color, tone, pattern, and scale
Curating your choices into a quilt can be difficult. It is where many people feel confused, because they are not used to making so many fabric choices. Instinctively, there will be a look and feel that you like, so just go with that. It may not be what everyone else likes, but that really doesn't matter.

When it comes to color, use Mother Nature as a guide—birds, gardens, and landscapes give you a really good idea of what works well together. Visit art galleries, look into store windows and florist shops, and look at books on anything but quilts to give you ideas. You might be stimulated by a Monet or a Rothko painting, or even a lighting installation. I have been inspired by everything from a book on fashion designer Vionnet to a walled garden in late autumn. Let your mind wander and enjoy coming up with a color palette you love. When choosing color combinations, just add and subtract fabrics to see how the overall look changes. Take your time, as this is an incredibly important part of making your quilt.

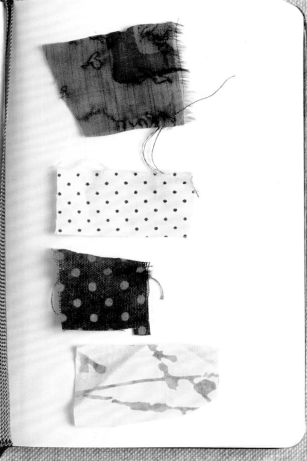

Another key aspect is the use of pattern and scale. I think of patterns in terms of three levels of scale. First, big or dominant patterns—huge flowers or birds, or fabric that has a repeat of, for example, a large poodle. Then medium patterns—leaves, smaller flowers, or toile. Lastly, there are the non-patterns—plain or textured fabrics, or those with repeated spots or stripes. Look at fabric collections and you will see how designers work all three scales into a range. If you are going to use big-scale patterns in your quilt, you really need to include the other two categories of pattern as well, to provide balance. They frame the larger-scale fabrics and highlight them, so they can really be seen. Mixing all three together helps your eye move across the quilt.

Calculating fabric quantities

The fabric quantities you need will vary, depending on the style of quilt you are making, as well as the finished size. Small pieces mean more seams, which means that more fabric will be needed.

First decide on the size of quilt you wish to make, then you can do a rough calculation. For example, a quilt with a finished size of 83 x 83in (210 x 210cm) means a total surface of 4¾yd (4.41m). I would then round this up by at least 1.25, which gives me 6yd (5.5m), to make sure that you have enough fabric to choose from. This may seem a little extravagant, but if you think about how much work is going to go into this quilt and how long you are going to have it, it no longer seems extravagant.

How many clothing garments do I need to make a quilt?

If you are a lover of 1950s-style prom skirts, you won't need many skirts to make a quilt. However, if you are making a quilt out of children's clothes, then you will need a lot more. If your husband's shirts are size XL, then you will need fewer than if they are size S.

It also depends on what style of quilt you are making—as in, how many seams and what size of pieces you are using.

Is the clothing you want to use to be a highlight of your quilt only, or do you want your quilt to be a medley of garments? Planning this out before you start your quilt will help you decide on how much clothing and/or extra fabric you need.

It is best to start by gathering together all the clothes you want to use in your quilt and laying them down on a bed or the floor to get a visual idea of how much you have. You will always need more clothing than off-the-roll fabric for a quilt, as the awkward shapes often result in quite a bit of wastage. Err on the generous side and if you don't think you have enough clothing, it is a great opportunity to go shopping for some new/old fabric to tie it together. If you have any left over, you can always use it for the backing or binding.

Shopping for fabric

When I am making a quilt I often create a mood board to get the idea of the quilt in my head. Often I have postcards from exhibitions or images that I have scanned from books as the starting point. At the very least, I load up a notebook with snips of the fabric I already have (see opposite). When I go shopping, I just open the book and see if any new fabric works with what is already planned.

If you are buying from a bolt of fabric, I suggest buying at least half a yard (or meter). If this is more than you think you will use for the quilt top, you can always use it up on the backing, but you need to make sure you have enough. Obviously, scarves, scraps, or dresses come as they are, and you will have to work with that.

Preparing fabrics

You don't want your quilt to pucker or run when you first clean it, so wash and press all the fabric before you use it, and wash it all separately. Hand-wash any fabrics that are delicate or of unknown provenance. Machine-wash the fabric if it has been commercially manufactured.

Washing removes the shrinkage in fabric. All cloth has different shrinkage, depending on how it is woven; hand-woven fabric is likely to shrink more. You also need to make sure there is no excess dye in the fabric, especially ethnic or hand-dyed fabric. Wash all your fabric separately until the water is clear. Some types of fabric dyes may need to be set by boiling the fabric in salted water. Lastly, some commercially produced fabric has a gelatine-like size on it, which makes the fabric look a bit tighter and firm. Once you wash it, this finish will disappear.

Before you start cutting your pieces, make sure everything has been pressed. If you are using clothing, remove collars, waistbands, and cuffs (see page 124), so that you have usable pieces of cloth, and then press well.

Threads

I love to use cotton thread—usually Coats cotton, but I'll use any cotton thread that I can get my hands on. Cotton thread sews smoothly, feels lovely when hand-quilting, and has an almost perfect level of sheen. I suggest you purchase a couple of different brands and see what you like the feel of. Designer Mies van der Rohe said "God is in the details," and you do not want your choice of thread to let the quilt down—I promise, it does make a difference. Use a neutral color for piecing, unless the fabrics are very dark.

If you are hand-quilting, your choice of thread color can add another level of personality to your quilt, so think about this at the planning stage.

Don't forget that you can use silk embroidery thread, linen thread, or wool for hand-quilting, too.

Tools and equipment

There aren't many special tools that you need to make a quilt, but having the key items will make life a lot easier and the act of making a quilt a great deal quicker. You can buy all of the equipment you need online or at a quilting store or good craft store.

The first three pieces of equipment below are specifically for making quilts. The others are items you would use for any sewing project.

Cutting mat (1)

A cutting mat simply protects your table or work surface when you are cutting fabric with a rotary cutter, and it also provides a grid for you to line up your fabric. They are available in many sizes and come marked with either imperial or metric measurements, or both, so make sure you buy the right kind for you.

A cutting mat can also be used for lots of other crafts, so it is an investment worth making.

Rotary cutter (2)

This is used to cut fabric on your cutting mat, together with a quilter's ruler—the third essential tool. It makes cutting fabric so much easier—it will change your quilting life.

The blade must always be moved away from your body when you are cutting, and always put the protective cover back over the blade when you have finished. Remember, a rotary cutter is, in fact, a circular razor blade, so it needs to be treated with respect.

You can buy rotary cutters in different sizes, and my preferred brand is Olfa, but the main thing is to find a cutter that feels comfortable in your hand. Don't forget to buy some spare blades and make sure you replace the blade regularly.

Quilter's ruler (3)

The last of the three key tools, a quilter's ruler is used to ensure that you cut the right-sized pieces. Made from transparent acrylic, it is designed to be used with a rotary cutter and cutting mat to make it easy to cut fabric accurately. Quilter's rulers come in a variety of sizes and are either metric or imperial. You will need one at least 12in (30cm) long, although longer is better.

Sewing machine

This doesn't need to be expensive, it just needs to be able to sew straight stitches. If you are machine-quilting, you will need a walking foot and a variety of needles, depending on the type of fabric you are using.

Make sure you have a ½in (1cm) seam marker on your machine. If you don't, use masking tape to mark a ½in (1cm) line to the right of your needle to use as your guide.

Iron

Use an iron with a steam option for perfectly pressed seams.

Pins

I find that long, fine pins are the best. Make sure they have glass or metal heads, as plastic heads will melt if they come into contact with a hot iron.

Scissors (4 and 5)

You will need fabric scissors (4), which should never be used for cutting paper, and a pair of small scissors (5) to cut threads.

Seam ripper (6)

This is useful for rectifying mistakes, enabling you to unpick seams very quickly. Make sure the blade is sharp.

Fabric chalk or erasable pencils (7)

Either of these can be used for tracing quilting designs onto fabric, if necessary.

Needles

Have a variety of needles for quilting or hand-stitching.

Thimbles

I prefer leather thimbles to metal ones, as I find them more flexible and comfortable.

Fusible interfacing

This is used to stabilize knits and fine or delicate fabrics.

Cutting and piecing

A note on cutting up garments

The thought of cutting up your wedding dress, baby's first dress, or any other garment is probably a little distressing. Once you start, there is, of course, no going back. However, once you have mustered the courage, this is the best way to approach each type of garment.

- Shirts—cut the sleeves off first and remove the cuffs. Then remove the collar. Cut along the seam lines of the fronts and back and remove any buttons or buttonhole sections. Finally, remove the placket, if the shirt has one (most men's shirts do). You are then left with flat pieces of fabric.

- Skirts—simply cut away the waistbands, inset pockets, and zippers. Then cut down the seam lines and voilà—plenty of usable fabric.

- Pants and shorts—cut off waistbands, inset pockets, and zippers. Then cut along each seam to create four flat pieces of fabric.

Cutting (1)

Although I like the idea of wabi-sabi in many things, cutting fabric for your quilt is not the right place to introduce the concept of "not-quite-perfect." If you cut your fabric accurately, you have a far greater chance of everything fitting perfectly when you sew the pieces together.

Make sure you work with pieces of fabric that are an appropriate size for your cutting mat. Cut anything large down to a manageable size before you start cutting your pieces.

Following the diagram of your chosen design, and starting with piece number 1, cut your first piece of fabric using your quilter's ruler as your size guide. Use the lines on your cutting mat to make sure that your fabric is sitting straight, but use the ruler to cut the correct size.

When cutting, make sure that the blade of the rotary cutter is perpendicular against the ruler, and always roll it away from you, pushing firmly but gently. If you need to, turn the cutting mat rather than yourself, and don't be tempted to cut across the fabric. Standing up when cutting makes it a lot easier.

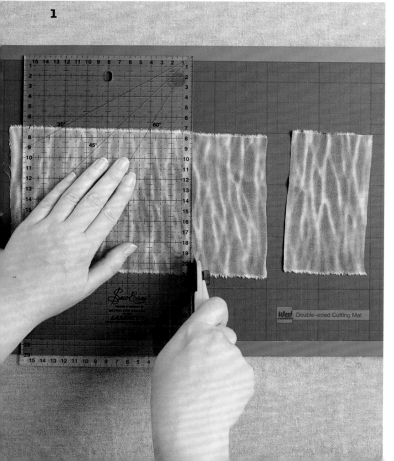

Last but not least, as a left-hander, I understand that many crafts are almost impossible to learn. (Knitting anyone?) With cutting, if you are left-handed, just use the left-hand side of the cutting mat as your reference point and hold your ruler in place with your right hand. If you are right-handed, use the right-hand side of the cutting mat as your starting point and hold the ruler with your left hand.

To fuss or not to fuss

The quilting term "fussy cutting" sounds terrible, but means something lovely. If you have a piece of fabric that has a bird or flower as a central motif, or some embroidery, you may want to cut the fabric to make the most of that. When cutting, use your quilter's ruler to center the motif. If it helps, use an erasable pencil or chalk to work this out accurately.

Piecing (2–4)

If you are making a quilt where all the pieces are similar sizes—such as the "Joining Together Quilt" on page 40—then cut all your pieces before you begin sewing them together. If they aren't, you may want to cut and piece the quilt top a section, or block, at a time, and then join them together.

Piecing is simply sewing all the different pieces in your quilt top together. You can piece by machine or hand. Piecing by machine is obviously a lot faster, but some projects are more practical to hand-piece—such as the "Keepsake Artworks" on page 110.

Join each piece with right sides together, in the order of the numbering shown on the diagram you are following. Pin the seam together before stitching it. Once you have sewn each piece in place, make sure you press the seam open with a steam iron. Pressing each seam as you go makes the finished quilt far more beautiful and will help you keep your sewing accurate. Turn the work and join on the next piece, gradually building up the block.

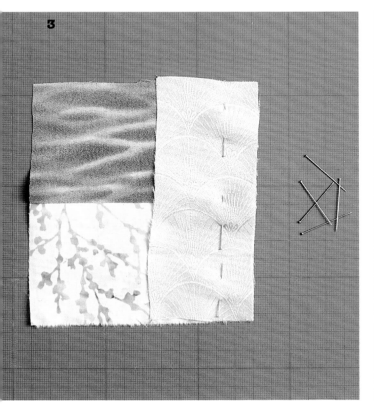

The parts of a quilt

A quilt is made up of four parts: the patchwork quilt top, the batting, which gives the thickness and warmth, the backing, and the binding. All four parts give you the option to create a quilt that is right for you and yours.

Quilt top

This is what you put the most work into and the part of the quilt that everyone sees. It is the design you choose and the fabric choices you make here that set everything else up.

Batting (below left)

Sometimes known as wadding, batting is the bit in the middle that gives weight to the quilt and keeps you warm.

There are numerous types of batting that you can use—from polyester to soy. There are cotton and cotton blends, such as a cotton/bamboo mix, and wool.

Some are loftier, some are easier to hand-quilt and some don't like sewing machines very much. It is best to look up "quilt batting" on the Internet and read about each type in detail to help you decide what you would like to use. I use either cotton or a cotton/bamboo mix, depending on the quilt and who it is for. I never use polyester batting.

You can also use other fabrics instead of batting. Indian kantha quilts use lots of layers of cotton to thicken the quilt. You could use an old wool blanket or fleece, or even woolen coat fabric. The point of batting is to keep you warm and add weight and substance to your quilt, so you can use any one of these options.

Always check the batting manufacturer's instructions to see if you need to wash the batting before you use it.

Quilt backing (opposite and below)

I like to think of the backing as the special surprise in a quilt. Nobody expects anything distinctive from the back, but it is the opportunity to turn the quilt into something quite special. The backing is the part of the quilt that you will feel the most and you want it to feel lovely, so I strongly recommend that you use a natural fabric for your backing.

As for what you can use, well, the list is almost endless. Antique sheets and hand-loomed cotton are great choices. How about the scraps from your quilt top, pieced together in a more random fashion? You can definitely buy lovely quilting cotton for your backing, but you could also use a sari or two, some soft cotton corduroy, or a light velvet. Don't use anything with stretch in it, though, unless you don't mind interfacing it first.

Binding

The edges of the quilt are enclosed in binding, so, on a practical level, it keeps the quilt durable. From a design perspective, the binding is another opportunity to add something special to tie everything together.

You can use many fabrics for your binding—scraps from the quilt top, a completely new piece of fabric, men's ties, or silk taffeta would all be lovely. You can also buy binding pre-made in everything from satin to Liberty cotton and velvet.

If you are making your own binding, it can either be cut across the straight grain of the fabric or on the bias. Cutting it on the straight grain is more economical and a little simpler to cut and piece together. Cutting the binding on the bias gives it some stretch, which makes it easier to ease around corners. (See also page 132.)

Quilt layout and assembly

Making the sandwich
Once you have made your quilt top and backing, you can put together your "quilt sandwich."

As mentioned in each project, your batting and backing both need to be at least 4in (10cm) larger all round than the quilt top. This is really important, because as you start pinning your quilt together, your quilt top will move slightly and it is better to have excess backing that you can trim, rather than cutting into your quilt top.

Press your backing and lay it right side down, preferably on a hard surface like the floor, or a table if it is a small quilt. Make sure the surface is really clean and that there is no chance of pets or children appearing at any point in this process. If you have made the backing out of a mixture of fabric, decide which is the top and bottom—that is, the direction it will be on the bed. Smooth out the backing carefully, so that there are no creases. Then, using masking tape, tape the backing to the surface at several points along each side but not at the corners.

Lay your batting on top and smooth it out, aligning the edges with the backing. If your batting is bigger than your backing, trim it down to match.

Press your quilt top until it is perfect, doing a final check for any loose threads as you go. Decide which is the top and bottom, then lay the quilt top right side up on top of the batting. Make sure the quilt top is square with the batting and backing, and smooth it out. You will have been on your knees for some time now, so you may want to take a break before the next part.

Pinning/Basting (opposite)
You now need to hold the three layers together so that you can quilt it. There are three options.

The first is to use pins, which is what I do—the longest you can find. Start from either the center or one side of the quilt and pin through all three layers every 6–8in (15–20cm), smoothing it out as you go. It is really important

to keep smoothing the quilt, otherwise you will get little gathers or excess fabric where you don't want it.

The advantage of using pins is that they are cheap, easy to use, and they allow you to use any method of quilting. The downside is that some will fall out and you will prick yourself as you hand-quilt your quilt—probably a fair bit. When I hand-quilt, I keep the quilt in a basket and do a sweep of the sofa once I have finished for the evening. This avoids many yelps from the family the next day.

The second option is to hand-baste/tack the quilt using (preferably but not essentially) a curved needle. You need to baste long stitches, about 4½–6in (12–15cm) apart both horizontally and vertically. You could get a long-arm quilter to do this for you (see Long-arm quilting below). The downside is that you can't machine-quilt a quilt that has been basted.

The third option is to use quilter's safety pins, which look like old-fashioned diaper pins and can be bought at quilting stores. Use the same technique as for pins. I am not so keen on this method, as it can make the quilt a little lumpy if you are a novice at this, and it also means that you have to pre-plan your quilting lines if you are intending to machine-quilt the quilt.

Tip for planning your quilting lines
Masking tape is a great tool in quilting, not just for when you are building your sandwich, but you can also use it to lay out straight lines on your quilt to follow when you are hand-quilting. Who would have thought?

Long-arm quilting
You can have your quilt long-arm quilted by very skilful and talented professionals. This is an option instead of hand- or machine-quilting the quilt yourself (see page 131). Instead of preparing the quilt sandwich yourself, you simply send the parts of your quilt to them, or make an appointment to visit. They can just baste the quilt for you, or fully quilt it and even sew on the binding. It is completely your choice as to how much of the process they do for you.

Long-arm quilting gives a flatter and more refined finish than hand-quilting and more precise designs than it is possible to achieve by machine-quilting on a domestic sewing machine. They also offer a huge variety of quilting designs and thread color options that add to the feel of your quilt. Usually, they can provide the batting, too, which will save you sourcing it.

I use long-arm quilters for all my commissioned quilts. They also basted several of the hand-quilted quilts in this book, because preparing the sandwich is my least favorite part of making a quilt.

We all have different combinations of time, money, and inclination, so you can use a long-arm quilting service to the level that suits you best.

Quilting

You have taped, layered, smoothed, and pinned (or you have sent it off for some other lovely person to do), and now you are ready to actually quilt. Again, there are many options here and each will give your quilt a different feel. The point of quilting is simply to hold the layers of the quilt together. The stitching can be very simple or highly decorative, you can apply rigid lines or be freeform in your style.

Long-arm quilting (see also pages 128–9)

I love this method because of how your choice of quilting design can completely change the feel of the whole quilt. It does tend to flatten the quilt and is probably more modern in feel, but I like this. I also like the fact that it gives you the opportunity to collaborate with artisans—and often that makes the finished quilt even better.

Hand-quilting

This method gives a completely different feel. It is much softer and your quilt will be bouncier and look more vintage. It will, of course, feel far more handmade, as your stitching lines will be broken rather than running together.

Sometimes I do like to hand-quilt and, if I do, I simply use a running stitch in the design of my choice. Often I just quilt ¼in (5mm) away from the seams, following my piecing lines; sometimes I quilt "in the ditch" (along the seams) for a more subtle feel; I also quilt around particular emblems or do more intricate lines—wiggly, wavy, whatever takes my fancy. I don't necessarily pre-plan how much and where I am going to quilt, but it varies, depending on the style of quilt that I have made.

The point is that you can hand-quilt as much as you like. You can spend 10 or 100 hours on it. I have a quilt that I have been working on for around six months. I hand-quilted enough straight lines to hold it all together and now that I have taken the pins out, I just keep adding a little more stitching whenever I feel like it. I hope I will know when to stop.

Traditional hand-quilters like to use hoops—freestanding or hand-held—as this keeps the quilt taut. Generally, I just quilt in my lap, starting from one side of the quilt and working across it, keeping it smooth as I go. Purists may not approve, but often I will just pick it up and quilt a bit I like the look of.

Machine-quilting

My least favorite method, machine-quilting doesn't have the beautiful simplicity of hand-quilting, nor the flair of long-arm quilting. It does have its place, though—if you want to make something quickly, for example, or if you want a really simple design. If you are a whizz on a sewing machine, you can tackle free-motion quilting, where you can create similar patterns to long-arm quilting.

If you have a simple domestic sewing machine, you will be restricted on how big a quilt you can machine-quilt: 63 x 63in (160 x 160cm) fits well, but I find it trickier to do anything larger than that. To make it easier to machine-quilt a large quilt, roll up one side of the quilt tightly so that it fits into the circular gap of your machine. Quilt as much as you can on one side and then turn it around, roll up the other side, and continue quilting.

Remember to use a walking foot for machine-quilting and a darning foot if you are skilled enough to take on free-motion quilting.

Other methods

Last but not least, you can use decorative buttons or beads to hold a quilt together, or some simple cross-stitches, as seen on the "I Love You Quilted Throw" on page 48. You could also hand-tie through the three layers using wool or cotton in a color of your choice.

These are much simpler methods of holding a quilt together and do look a little naive, but for the right project any of them can look fantastic. These methods also let you introduce a different kind of thread or object to your quilt. Just remember who it is for and make sure that it will be functional as well as looking lovely.

Binding

Once you have quilted your quilt, trim away all the excess backing and batting, so that these layers are even with the quilt top and you have straight lines (see below left). Be careful not to over-trim—it is easy to be over-zealous about perfect lines, to the point where parts of the top disappear between your scissors or under your rotary cutter.

There are more ways to bind a quilt than you can imagine and everyone is passionate about their own method. I like fine narrow binding, some like sturdy wide binding. I love neatly spaced slipstitching, but this will be water torture for some of you.

Experiment with different methods until you find one you like. You can use someone else's method for attaching binding if it suits you better. Or last, but definitely not least, you can hand it back to the lovely long-arm quilters and they will do it for you.

Making the binding

Measure all four sides of your quilt and add on another 6–8in (15–20cm) to get the length of binding required.

You can, of course, use ready-made binding, but if you want to make it yourself, first select your binding fabric (see page 126). You need to cut it in strips, either across the grain or on the bias. Cutting strips on the bias creates binding with more give but it uses up more fabric.

I usually cut the strips approximately 2in (5cm) wide because I like narrow binding, but you can make them a different width if you want wider binding. Remember to include a ½in (1cm) seam allowance when deciding on the width of the strips.

Join all the strips together end to end, with rights sides facing, to form a continuous length long enough to go all the way around your quilt. Then press the strip in half along its length, with wrong sides together, to form a central crease.

Attaching the binding

Attaching binding is difficult to describe—I have read many versions and they always leave me even more perplexed. I asked my mother to show me how she does it, and so that is how I have always done it.

Leave about 4in (10cm) of one end of the binding strip free. Then, with right sides together, start pinning one raw edge of the binding to the edge of the quilt (opposite, below right). Pin all the way around the quilt, through all layers, until you reach your starting point. Leave the ends of the binding free.

Machine-stitch the binding in place around the edge of the quilt. There are more ways to deal with corners than you can imagine. Some people like to attach binding one side at a time, starting each side with a new strip and folding the second strip over the first corner, and so on. My preferred method is to stop sewing about ¼in (5mm) from the corner, backstitch, and then fold the binding around the corner—but that is because I like a rounder corner and you may prefer sharp corners.

When you near your starting point, backstitch, and remove the quilt from the sewing machine. Trim off the excess tails of binding, leaving enough to hem the ends. Fold the ends under and overlap one end of the binding with the other. Pin in place, then sew the last few stitches.

Fold the binding over to the back of the quilt and pin it in place with the raw edge turned under. Hand-stitch the binding to the quilt backing using a slipstitch, so that the stitching is invisible.

Note: You can try to machine-stitch the binding to the front and back of the quilt in one go. You will need lots of pins and a careful eye to make sure that you catch all the layers within the stitching.

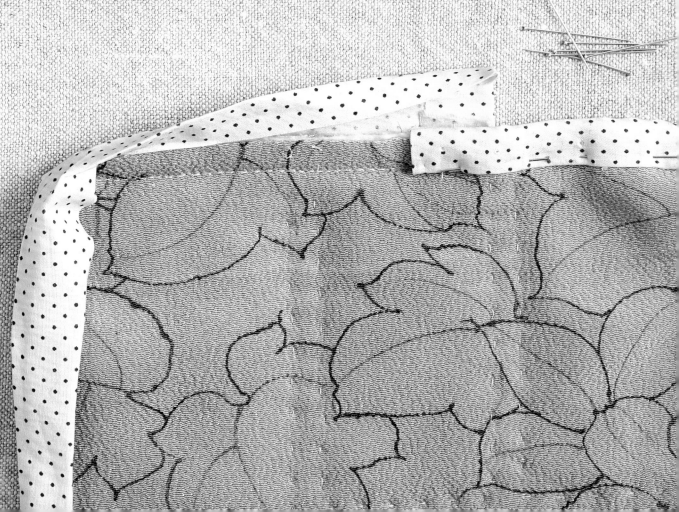

How to create your own designs— freestyling

This is where it all began for me. I loved quilts and what they stood for, but I didn't like what was available. I felt oppressed and a little confused in quilting stores. Everything seemed so restrictive—use this fabric combination, in this method, in this design. What if I didn't like some of the fabric in the set? What if I wanted to use my beloved Japanese silks?

So, once I learned how to make a quilt (thanks, again, to my mother), I simply made one in my own design. I call this freestyling. It is not hard and it is incredibly liberating. All you need is a bit of inspiration, sketching paper, graph paper, tracing paper, a pencil and eraser, and a scale rule. That's it—oh, and a bit of basic math.

To come up with ideas, visit galleries, stores, and gardens. Take in an exhibition or two and read books on anything that interests you. I will come clean and admit that I own only three practical quilting books and one historical book on quilts and quilting—I realize that isn't a lot. But I do own about 500 books on textiles, art, poetry, design, gardens, typography, travel, and fashion. This is where my inspiration comes from. A Robert Frost poem gave me a fantastic idea for a quilt design, and images from ethnic textile books have given me many others. A contemporary book on flowers started the color palettes for at least two quilts in this book and an old cookbook from New Zealand another. You can find inspiration absolutely anywhere. Don't be restricted by what you think you should do.

Once you are suitably inspired, sketch something or lots of things, make a mood board, or take some photographs. Decide on the shape and size of your quilt, and then you are ready to design a pattern.

Decide on the scale you need to use. If you have never used a scale ruler before, pop into your local art store and let them explain how to use it. If you are making a queen-size quilt, then the best scale is 1:5 if you are working in imperial. This means that 1in on the graph paper equals 5in in real life, and your diagram will fit on a piece of tabloid-size (11 x 17in) graph paper. If you are working in metric, use a scale of 1:10, where 1cm on the graph paper equals 10cm in real life. By scaling your quilt design down, you are able to draw it up in a manageable size. The image opposite is just that. This drawing was the starting point for the "Special Birthday Quilt" on page 22.

Using a pencil, start transferring your sketch into an actual design onto your graph paper. Remember to draw it so that you can build blocks when you cut and piece the quilt together. This means that each piece must be the same length or width as the piece you are joining it to on that seam. Look at the other diagrams in the book to remind you.

Move your lines around until you have a completed design you are happy with. Then you need to mark the finished size and cutting size on each piece on the diagram. The finished size is the dimensions you have drawn and represents the sewn patch on the finished quilt. The cutting size is what you actually need to cut out—the finished size with the seam allowance added around all four sides (including those on the edges of the quilt). I always use a seam allowance of ½in (1cm), firstly because it makes the math simpler and secondly because it makes it easier to incorporate different fabrics and also allows for less-than-perfect stitching if you are a beginner; but this is your chance to use a seam allowance that you are comfortable with. As an example, if my finished piece is 8 x 12in (20 x 30cm) and my seam allowance is ½in (1cm), then my cutting size will be 9 x 13in (22 x 32cm).

Trace the design and mark in the cutting size only. If you wish, you can color in fabric choices, or take the diagram with you when you are purchasing fabrics. Your design may have come from fabrics you already have, which is just as exciting.

This is what I want you all to be able to do—create your own quilt. One that says: "This is me, this is my life, this is my story." If any of you do this, it would make me very happy indeed. We will have come full circle and quilt making will be about personal expression and family and history, whatever yours may be.

You can find INSPIRATION absolutely *anywhere*. Don't be restricted by what you think you *should do*.

Resources

There are many, many quilting fabric stores around the world, both on and offline. Since I live in the UK, I wanted to provide a few of my favorites—places where you can buy artisan cloth or fabric not normally used for quilting. I've also provided a few resources suggested by the Taunton Press, my publisher in the United States.

AUTHOR'S RESOURCES

The Cloth House, London, England
www.clothhouse.com
This store is my favorite place to buy fabrics. Every quilt in this book has fabric from The Cloth House in it.

Liberty of London, London, England
www.liberty.co.uk
Higher price cottons, but the quality is exceptional and the colors and designs are amazing.

MacCulloch & Wallis, London, England
www.macculloch-wallis.co.uk
Wonderful silks and shirting cottons.

The Cloth Shop, London, England
www.theclothshop.net
Specializing in antique fabrics, French and Swedish linens, cotton velvets, and more. Unfortunately, they don't sell over the Internet.

Sri threads, Brooklyn, New York, USA
www.srithreads.com
Perfect for something very special from Japan or India.

Russell and Chapple, London, England
www.russellandchapple.co.uk
Excellent quality linens and cottons for a very good price. The tote bag linen came from here.

Fabrics Galore, London, England
www.fabricsgalore.co.uk
They sell Liberty fabrics at discount, as well as a whole host of other great fabrics.

Ichiroya
www.ichiroya.com
Kimono nirvana. If you like Japanese cloth, you will find what you want here, either in bolts, kimonos, or pieces.

African Fabric store
www.africanfabric.co.uk
A fantastic selection of African fabric. Some of the fabrics for the Joining Together and Backyard Picnic quilts, as well as the tote bag, came from here.

Clothaholics
www.clothaholics.com
Japanese fabrics—sign up for the newsletter for sale and new stock notices.

Organic Cotton
www.organiccotton.biz
A huge selection of organic knit and woven fabric in various weights and lovely colors.

Parna
www.parna.co.uk
An excellent selection of vintage linen sheets for quilt backings.

Ebay/Etsy
www.ebay.com and www.etsy.com
Just put in what you think you want and hundreds, if not thousands, of sellers will pop up.

Antiques Fairs
Puce in Paris, Ardingly in the UK, Brooklyn Flea in New York and Brimfield Antique Show in Brimfield, Massachusetts, USA. There are, in fact, many, many fairs and markets that offer textiles.

Second Hand/Charity Stores
Some are awful, some are fantastic: buy things you like and stash them away.

Last but definitely not least—You
Quilts can tell stories and they can gather together you and your family's story. So look through your cupboards and boxes and gather up your travel memorabilia. Talk to your family and gather precious cloth from them. You'll be amazed at what you find and what you'll be able to turn into your own heirloom.

ADDITIONAL RESOURCES

ACMoore, USA
www.acmoore.com
Sewing supplies, fabrics, needlearts, and crafts.

Clotilde, USA
www.clotilde.com
Quilting, sewing, fabric, and notions.

Fabric Shoppers Unite
www.fabricshoppersunite.com
A worldwide network of independent quilt and fabric shops, e-tailers and design studios.

Fabricland, North Plainfield, New Jersey, USA
www.fabricland.com
Dress and quilting fabrics, decorative fabrics and supplies.

Fabricville, Montreal and Quebec, Canada
www.fabricville.com
Home decor and fashion fabrics and notions.

Hobby Lobby, USA
www.hobbylobby.com
Fabrics, ribbons, buttons, sewing notions, and trims.

JoAnn Fabric Stores, USA
www.JoAnn.com
A large assortment of fabric, sewing, and quilting supplies.

Purl Soho, New York, New York, USA
www.purlsoho.com
Fabric, precut bundles, precut fabric, and more.

Inspirations

There are places and books that continue to inspire me, no matter how many times I visit or read them. I have mentioned before that I don't have a lot of books on quilts, but all the books and places below have been the trigger for at least one design or thought. Visit as many exhibitions and galleries as you can. Look at movies and costumes as reference points. Enjoy gardens at all times of the year—in winter I think they are at their most sculptural and artistic. Let these places and books fill you up and spark ideas for color, line, or even a completely new design.

PLACES

Charleston

Firle, Lewes, East Sussex BN8 6LL
+44 (0)1323 811 626
www.charleston.org.uk
I like to think of Charleston as "my place," but I am sure thousands of others do, too. It was the home and country meeting place for the writers, painters, and intellectuals known as the Bloomsbury Group. It is where I feel most inspired, not just by what they created, but also by the thought of how individual you can be.

V & A

Cromwell Road, London SW7 2RL
+44 (0)20 7942 2000
www.vam.ac.uk
Described as the world's greatest museum of art and design, the V&A is extraordinary. Textiles, clothing, architecture, metalwork, jewelry—this list goes on. It is a vibrant and exciting museum that feels alive. Entry is free, except for special exhibitions, and these are usually well worth the ticket price.

Kelmscott Manor

Kelmscott, Lechlade, Glos, GL7 3HJ
+44 (0)1367 252486
www.kelmscottmanor.org.uk
Kelmscott was the summer home of William Morris and is probably his most evocative house. It contains an outstanding collection of the possessions and works of Morris, his family and associates, including furniture, original textiles, pictures, carpets, ceramics, and metalwork.

Rothko room at the Tate Modern

Tate Modern, Bankside, London SE1 9TG
+44 (0)20 7887 8888
www.tate.org.uk/modern
I find Mark Rothko's paintings incredibly inspiring, and this permanent room at the Tate Modern is well worth a visit.

Riba Bookshops

www.ribabookshops.com
There are three locations in London (Portland Place is my favorite). I find books on architecture a great resource when designing quilts. It is something about construction mixed with creativity that helps me. To look at the works of some of the greats can set your mind racing in all sorts of directions.

Barbara Hepworth Museum & Sculpture Garden

Barnoon Hill, St Ives, Cornwall TR26 1AD
www.tate.org.uk/visit/tate-st-ives/barbara-hepworth-museum
To visit this place is a unique experience, offering a remarkable insight into Barbara Hepworth's work. Sculptures in bronze, stone, and wood are on display in the museum and garden, along with paintings, drawings, and archive material.

Sissinghurst Castle

Biddenden Road, near Cranbrook, Kent TN17 2AB
+44 (0)1580 710 701
www.nationaltrust.org.uk/sissinghurst-castle/
I visit a lot of gardens, but Sissinghurst is my favorite. I love places that are the creative vision of one person and I think that Vita Sackville-West may have been a very interesting person to meet. Her garden legacy will have to do. Try and visit it at different times of the year, as this is when you will see how very, very clever she was.

BOOKS & MAGAZINES

I could list hundreds, but these books and magazines are always on standby.

Etcetera and Nomad, Sibella Court
Flair Annual 1953, Random House
Grandiflora Arrangements, Saskia Havekes and Gary Heery
Home is where the heart is? and *Sensual Home*, Ilse Crawford
Madeleine Vionnet, Betty Kirke
Minimum, John Pawson
Poiret, The Metropolitan Museum of Art
Quilting, Patchwork and Appliqué—A world guide, Caroline Crabtree and Christine Shaw
The Quilts of Gee's Bend: Masterpieces from a Lost Place, William Arnett
Textiles: A World Tour, Catherine Legrand
Unwrapped, Carolyn Quartermaine

Bloom (Li Edelkoort)
Come Home (Japan)
Hand/Eye Magazine (US)
Vogue Living (Australia)
World of Interiors (UK)

Directory

On the following pages is a directory of all the projects featured in the book, ranging from gorgeous full-size quilts to smaller throws and other quick-to-make items such as a table runner, pillow, and framed artwork.

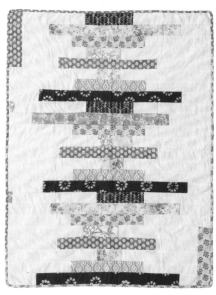

New Baby Quilt 10

Marriage Quilt 16

Special Birthday Quilt 22

Leaving The Nest Quilt 28

Fresh Start Quilt 34

Joining Together Quilt 40

I Love You Quilted Throw 48

Comfort And Care Quilt 52

Cheer Up A Loved One Table Runner 58

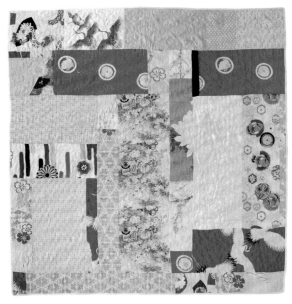

Favorite Fabric Quilt 62

Friendship Bracelet 68

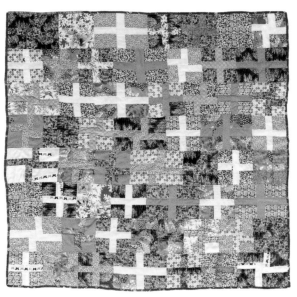

Morning Coffee Quilt Circle 70

Catch-All Reversible Tote 76

Housewarming Pillow 80

Pull Up A Pouffe 84

Backyard Picnic Quilt 88

Celebration Of Life Quilt 96

Keepsake Artworks 110

Traveler's Tales Quilt 104

Mementos Curtain Panel 112

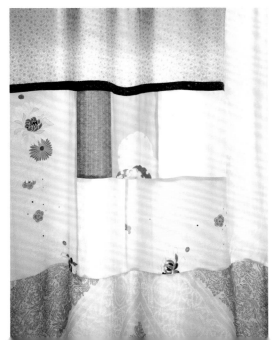

143

Acknowledgments

A huge thank you to

My incredibly talented mother, who put the needle and thread into my hands.
My sister, who waves the flag highest of all from the other side of the world.
Rache—for her gorgeous pictures and incredibly calm approach.
The clever ladies at The Quilt Room for perfect quilting and enthusiasm for
these kinds of quilts.
The whole team at Jacqui Small.
Di and Ivan, our friends and exceptionally helpful dog minders.
And my Ed, who is extraordinarily patient as well as just extraordinary.

PRESS CREDITS

The lovely Samuel Sparrow at **Sparrow and Co**, a new online collection
of beautifully made homewares: www.sparrowandco.com

Anthropologie UK: www.anthropologie.eu

Cologne & Cotton: mail order: 0845 262 2212; www.cologneandcotton.com

To place an order or to request a catalog, contact
The Taunton Press, Inc.
63 South Main Street, P.O. Box 5506, Newtown, CT 06470-5506
Tel (800) 888-8286

www.taunton.com